THE LORD'S HOUSE

A History of Sheffield's Roman Catholic Buildings 1570–1990

Denis Evinson

St Marie's Church, Sheffield

THE LORD'S HOUSE

A History of Sheffield's Roman Catholic
Buildings 1570–1990

Denis Evinson

Sheffield Academic Press

To my wife

Copyright © 1991 Sheffield Academic Press

Published by Sheffield Academic Press Ltd
The University of Sheffield
343 Fulwood Road
Sheffield S10 3BP
England

Typeset by Sheffield Academic Press
and
Printed on acid-free paper in Great Britain
by Billing & Sons Ltd
Worcester

British Library Cataloguing in Publication Data

Evinson, Denis
    The Lord's House: A History of Sheffield's Roman
    Catholic buildings. 1570–1990
    I. Title
    282.42821

ISBN 1-85075-303-2

CONTENTS

ILLUSTRATIONS

ILLUSTRATION ACKNOWLEDGMENTS AND SOURCES

Frontispiece, *The Builder* 1885; 2, 12, Hunter's *Hallamshire*; 3, 5, 8, Hadfield's *History of St Marie's*; 7, *The Builder* 1865; 9, 15, Royal Commission on the Historical Monuments of England; 10, 11, J.H. Langtry-Langton Partners; 13, Pugin's *Present State*; 14, *The Dublin Builder* 1860; 17, *British Architect* 1892; 20, British Architectural Library, RIBA, and *Architecture Illustrated* 1936; 34, John Mottershaw Photography, Mr V. Steinlet and *Church Building* 1990.

FOREWORD

It is with the greatest pleasure that I write a few words to introduce the reader to 'The Lord's House'.

The story of the development of the Catholic Church in Sheffield since the end of the eighteenth century is a fascinating one. But most of the details about it would have been lost forever had it not been for the painstaking research of Dr Denis Evinson.

With a pleasing style and economy of words he presents the reader with accurate information and detailed descriptions of church buildings in Sheffield and describes precisely the development of our parishes in Sheffield.

I warmly congratulate Dr Evinson on the production of this book, and I thank him for the time and work he has spent on it. In my opinion it is already a standard work and I hope that many people will ensure that they have a copy.

+ GERALD MOVERLEY
Bishop of Hallam

PREFACE

The form of this book has been dictated by the present state of our information on Sheffield's Catholic history. Since Hadfield's *History of St Marie's* (1889) there has been no major work touching the whole subject. It seemed desirable, therefore, to place at least the basic facts concerning all of Sheffield's Catholic foundations between the covers of one book.

I have organized the material on a chronological and parochial basis, with chapters on recusant times followed by others treating churches, chapels, schools, convents, homes and hospitals. The entries are not parish histories; they aim only to cover missionary foundations, building history, architectural matters, art work, patronage and priests. I venture to hope, however, that this work may serve as a useful starting point from which others may write studies in depth of their own churches, schools and other buildings.

In addition to Hadfield's book I have been able to draw upon jubilee and centenary accounts of various churches and schools. Also informative were certain ecclesiastical, architectural and local press files. These and general printed works consulted appear in the footnotes and in the bibliography.

For the early chapters I have been fortunate in possessing two sources not available to Hadfield when he wrote over a century ago. First, the financial papers relating to the Sheffield estates of the Dukes of Norfolk are now deposited in the Archives Division of Sheffield City Library, under the title of Arundel Castle Manuscripts. These have yielded much new information on The Lord's House and the Old Chapel. For permission to quote from them, I am grateful to His Grace the Duke of Norfolk, EM, CBE, MC, and to the Director of Libraries. The second new source is the manuscript diary of William Statham, which furnishes a lively impression of the recusant condition in the eighteenth century.

I am particularly grateful to the many friends and relations who have cushioned my note-taking and field-work visits to Sheffield with generous hospitality, all of whom wish to remain anonymous. I am grateful also to those others, too numerous to mention individually, who have taken a keen interest in the progress of the work since its inception. Many of them have suggested sources which have yielded valuable information.

Besides these, I am especially grateful to the following for specific information and assistance: Mr J. Campbell, Dr D.R. Cullen, Mr W. Driver, Mr T. Green, Mr A. Havenhand, Mrs Helen Hodges, Miss Angela Molloy, Dr J.M. Robinson and the late Professor Stephen Welsh.

Thanks are in order to those parish priests, heads of schools and other superiors of institutions, who have given of their time to answer questions, and allowed me to take photographs. Particularly helpful also were the archivists of the Hallam, Leeds and Nottingham Dioceses; of the English Province SJ; and of the Little Sisters of the Poor.

I am indebted additionally to the Librarians and their staffs at the following institutions:

Allen Hall (Westminster Diocesan Seminary)
The British Library
Catholic Central Library
Catholic Education Council
Fulham Library
Hammersmith Library
Royal Institute of British Architects
Sheffield City Library
University of London Library
University of Sheffield Library
Ushaw College

To all of these I am indeed grateful.

Finally, it remains to thank His Lordship Bishop Moverley for the approval and encouragement he has shown at various stages of the work. He has assisted thereby a long-cherished ambition to produce this book on Sheffield's Catholic history. May I venture to hope that the result is worthy of the subject; in doing so, I must add that responsibility for any errors belongs solely to the author.

Denis Evinson
Feast of Forty Martyrs of England and Wales 1990

ABBREVIATIONS

Anstruther	G. Anstruther, *The Seminary Priests*, 4 vols., 1968–77
Arundel	Arundel Castle Manuscripts, Archives Division, Sheffield City Library
BN	*Building News*
Br	*The Builder*
Cassidy	Barbara Cassidy, 'A History of Sheffield's Roman Catholic Schools', typescript, 1969
Cathedral	S.P. Sullivan and J. Ryan, *St Marie's Cathedral, A History and Guide*, 1988
Catholic Monthly	*St Marie's Catholic Monthly*
CBR.N	*Catholic Building Review* (Northern)
CBR.S	*Catholic Building Review* (Southern)
CD	Catholic Directory of England and Wales
Colvin	H. Colvin, *Biographical Dictionary of British Architects*, 2nd edn, 1978
CRS	*Catholic Record Society Transactions*, 1904–
de l'Hôpital	W. de l'Hôpital, *Westminster Cathedral and its Architect*, 2 vols., 1919
DNB	Dictionary of National Biography
Foley	Henry Foley, SJ, *Records of the English Province of the Society of Jesus*, 8 vols., 1877–1883
Gatty	Alfred Gatty, *Sheffield Past and Present*, 1873
Gillow	J. Gillow, *Bibliographical Dictionary of the English Catholics*, 5 vols., 1885–1898
Hadfield	Charles Hadfield, *A History of St Marie's Mission and Church*, Sheffield, 1889
HC	*The Hallamshire Catholic*, 1937–44
Hunter	Joseph Hunter, *Hallamshire*, 1875 edn
Jubilee	*Sacred Heart Church, 1936–1986, Golden Jubilee*
Kelly	B.W. Kelly, *Historical Notes on English Catholic Missions*, 1907
Pevsner	N. Pevsner, *Yorkshire, West Riding*, 2nd edn, 1967
SDT	*Sheffield Daily Telegraph*
SRI	*Sheffield and Rotherham Independent*
St Vincent's	*St Vincent's, Sheffield, 1853-1953*
Welsh	Stephen Welsh, Notes on the Architectural Firm of J.G. Weightman and M.E. Hadfield

Chapter 1

THE QUEEN AND THE MARTYRS

Catholic worship took place in the Parish Church of Saints Peter and Paul, and in the chapel of Our Lady of the Bridge in Sheffield, up to the death of Queen Mary I. Then under Queen Elizabeth, the 1559 Act of Uniformity abolished Catholic liturgy, and the Prayer Book superseded the Mass. In Sheffield, the Church Burgesses had the altars demolished and replaced by a table of wood. Subsequently, the rood screen was dismantled and sold, statues were disfigured, and the cross in the churchyard was demolished.[1]

In Sheffield as elsewhere throughout the kingdom, the majority conformed to the threat imposed by the royal *fait accompli*. Refusal to take the Oath of Supremacy could involve Catholics in confiscation of property, imprisonment, and possibly death. Following the Papal deposition of Elizabeth in 1570 and the threat of foreign invasion in the 1580s, further legislation against Catholics specified it as high treason to reconcile or be reconciled to Rome, and to be ordained a priest.[2]

Within this climate of reformed liturgy and anti-Papal opinion, the remnant of faithful Catholics, oppressed by penal laws, held on to their faith as best they could. The rank and file could do little to help themselves. They were aided, however, by Catholic nobility and landed gentry, who for two centuries maintained missions in secret, despite the regular discouragement of imprisonment and fines. None of this would have been possible without the clergy, especially the Jesuits and the seminary priests from Douay, who risked imprisonment and death in coming to England to minister to the faithful.

1. Hadfield, p. 5.
2. E.I. Watkin, *Roman Catholicism in England* (London: Oxford University Press, 1957), pp. 18-22.

The absence of Catholic observance in central Sheffield is thus more readily understood. In the meantime, lay–clerical collaboration at such outlying estates as Padley, Stannington, Bolsterstone and Spinkhill ensured that the light of the old faith was not completely extinguished in the district.

Mary Queen of Scots

At this point we should not pass to consideration of local recusants without first noting the sojourn in Sheffield of Mary Queen of Scots. Following her flight from her Scottish enemies, Mary sought help to recover her throne from her cousin Queen Elizabeth. She became, however, Elizabeth's helpless prisoner, detained by no legal right; for as heir-presumptive to the English throne, supported by the Pope, respected by Christian Europe and the focus of English Catholic preference, Mary represented a permanent threat to Elizabeth's security.

Elizabeth laid the task of gaoler on George Talbot, 6th Earl of Shrewsbury, Lord of the Manor of Sheffield. Shrewsbury was a nobleman of the first rank, loyal to the monarch and moderate in religion. He was extremely wealthy, with properties at Sheffield, Worksop, Wingfield, Rufford, Buxton and Tutbury. His countess held the estates of Chatsworth and Hardwick. Shrewsbury's wealth and the inland situation of his estates rendered him ideal as the keeper of the royal prisoner.[1]

Mary arrived in Sheffield in November 1570, and left for the last time in September 1584. Her principal prison was Sheffield Castle, but visits were made to Sheffield Manor and to Buxton, Chatsworth and Worksop. The castle, a spacious fortified building, occupied about four acres between Dixon Lane, Waingate and the rivers Sheaf and Don.[2]

The Manor had been built in the early 1500s as a hunting lodge in the deer park of the 4th Earl. Here Cardinal Wolsey had stayed for eighteen days on his journey from York to Leicester in 1529, where he died. The ruins of the Manor may still be visited, as well as the detached Turret House which Mary must have known. Stylistically, the Turret House belongs to the 1570s, and Shrewsbury may have referred to this when he wrote to Burghley in 1577, 'I have sent

1. *DNB*, vol. LV, pp. 314-15.
2. Gatty, p. 22.

Greves a plate [i.e. plan] of a front of a lodge that I am now in building, which if it were not for troubling your Lordship, I would wish your advice therein'.[1]

Plate 1 The Turret House, Sheffield Manor, 1577

Mary's retinue at Sheffield Castle consisted of about thirty attendants, mostly French and Scottish. Besides the ladies who attended her, she was allowed a physician, a secretary, a page, a food-taster and various menials.[2] But under these conditions of reasonably comfortable captivity Mary lacked above all the service of a regular chaplain. At Shrewsbury's castle at Tutbury, Sir John Morton, a Catholic priest, joined her staff but probably died soon afterwards.[3]

1. William Odom, *Mary Stuart, Queen of Scots* (Sheffield: J.W. Northend, 1904), p. 145; John D. Leader, *Mary Queen of Scots in Captivity* (Sheffield: Leader and Sons, 1880), p. 156.

2. Gatty, p. 49.

3. Antonia Fraser, *Mary Queen of Scots* (London: Weidenfeld and Nicolson,

Then Ninian Winzet, a Scottish priest who had been at Mary's court at Holyrood, left his post at the University of Paris and returned to her service. Described by Shrewsbury as 'her Scottish secretary', he was at Sheffield by May 1571, but was among those compelled to leave the queen's service when her household was reduced in numbers.[1]

It is doubtful that Shrewsbury was unaware of their priesthood. Unquestionably loyal to Queen Elizabeth, he was also kindly and tolerant towards his royal prisoner, probably turning a blind eye to these priests. For a sudden political upheaval, engendered by foreign arms, could conceivably end Elizabeth's reign and place Mary upon the English throne. So as far as he dared, Shrewsbury cultivated good relations with Mary. No trace is found, however, of official Catholic chaplains. In October 1571, Mary requested Elizabeth's permission to confer with one of her French servants, or one of the retinue of the French Ambassador, concerning the provision of a chaplain, and requested also permission to correspond with her son. Her letter was dated 'de mon estroite prison de Chefild' (from my narrow prison of Sheffield) 29 October 1571.[2]

Yet chapel furniture and artefacts were listed in an inventory of goods at Sheffield Castle and Lodge, taken in 1582. Among these we find:

> In the Queenes chambers—Imprimis hangings of the Passion and of warres, peces viii.
> Alter clothes—Item clothes of cloth of gold and russet velvett, ii.
> Vestements—Item vestements embrodered, i.
> Bybles: Item bybles, ii.
> > Item one book cont'ᵦ ye halfe collume of ye Actes and Monuments [i.e. Day Hours], i.
> Pulpytts—Item pulpytts of wood, i.[3]

Not listed in the inventory are such aids to devotion as personal

---

1969), pp. 487, 533. However, Dr M. Lynch suggests convincingly that this was James Myrton, a Scottish Jesuit; see *Records of the Scots Colleges* (Aberdeen: New Spalding Club, 1906), vol. I, p. 2.

1. T.H. Burns, 'Catholicism in Defeat', in *History Today* (Nov. 1966), pp. 790-93.

2. William Odom, *op. cit.*, p. 138.

3. The original among the Talbot papers in the College of Arms quoted in *British Archaeological Association Journal*, vol. 30 (1874), pp. 251ff.

rosaries, missals, scapularies and the ivory crucifix which Mary wore. No doubt these were at Worksop with the queen when the inventory was taken.

After a space of ten years apparently without a chaplain, Mary received three extended visits from the Jesuit Henri Samerie in the early 1580s. Under the alias of Girolamo Mertelli, Samerie came disguised as a physician, with a relief party of new servants. Mary's extant instructions to Samerie show that she wished the Pope and the French princes to learn of her conditions, including deprivation of the Mass and the free exercise of her religion. On his third visit, it is likely that Samerie brought with him another priest, Camille de Preau, who managed to remain in Mary's service under the guise of a valet or a reader to the end.[1]

De Preau's role as a secret chaplain was far from easy, as Mary was finally removed from Sheffield in September 1584, and handed over to Amyas Paulet, a guardian more malevolent than Shrewsbury. At the queen's execution, at Fotheringhay in 1587, de Preau was kept locked away until all was over. She had, however, a ciborium containing a consecrated host, which she administered to herself, a Papal dispensation granted her if denied the ministrations of a priest preparatory to her death.[2]

An inventory of the queen's goods at this time included rings, a tablet of enamelled gold containing a picture of the King and Queen of France, bracelets with a history of the Passion of Christ, and a Matins book with clasps of gold.[3]

The Padley Martyrs

The difficulties of the Queen of Scots' situation were if anything lighter than those of English recusants. Fines for non-attendance at church were common, and penalties of imprisonment, sequestration of property, and even death awaited those who aided priests. Rewards

1. J.H. Pollen, 'Mary Stuart's Jesuit Chaplain', in *The Month* (Jan. and Feb. 1911).

2. Agnes Strickland, *Life of Mary Queen of Scots* (London: G. Bell and Sons, 1873), vol. II, p. 448. Miss Strickland, incidentally, describes de Preau as the queen's almoner.

3. *Calendar of State Papers, Scotland* (Edinburgh: H.M. General Register Office, 1900), vol. II, p. 1019.

tempted informers against recusants, so that lay martyrs as well as clerical were not unknown.

What this could mean is illustrated by the events at Padley. The prospect of a Spanish invasion provoked the Privy Council to order the internment of provincial Catholics. As Lord Lieutenant, the Earl of Shrewsbury and a party of men raided Padley with the arrest of John Fitzherbert in view. Arrived there, they found two seminary priests, Nicholas Garlick and Robert Ludlam, whom they took to Derby. They were tried and sentenced to death, and together with another priest, Richard Simpson, were hanged, drawn and quartered at Derby on 24th July 1588.

John Fitzherbert was found guilty of harbouring the priests at Padley. He was thus liable to the death penalty, but was in fact kept in Derby gaol. After two years he was sent to the Fleet prison in London, dying there, it is said, of gaol fever in November 1590.[1]

Other Seminary Priests

Contemporary with the Padley martyrs is another seminary priest, James Clayton, of Sheffield. The son of a shoemaker, he was apprenticed for seven years to a sicklesmith and shearsmith. He was a convert and without education, but devoted his leisure to study, especially of Latin. He arrived at the English College at Rheims in January 1582 and studied Divinity, being ordained at Soissons in June 1584. Sent to England in April 1585, he landed at Newcastle and worked in his native locality. He was apprehended at Christmas 1588 while visiting Catholic prisoners in Derby gaol, and condemned to death for his priesthood. However, he died in July 1589, of the stench in the gaol.[2]

More fortunate was Richard Slack of Dronfield, seminary priest. He was ordained at Rheims in 1579 and sent to England. Arrested at Rothley, Leicestershire, he was committed to the Tower in 1582 and condemned in 1584, but not executed. Banished in 1585, he served as a chaplain in Lorraine and on the teaching staff at Rheims.[3]

1. Garrett Sweeney, *A Pilgrim's Guide to Padley* (Nottingham: Diocese of Nottingham, 1978); Anstruther, vol. I, p. 216.
2. Hadfield, p. 9; Anstruther, vol. I, p. 79.
3. Anstruther, vol. I, p. 318.

Lay Recusants

Such men as these may have served the local recusants in secret with Mass and the sacraments. For recusants there were, their names known to us from lists constructed in the Diocese of York. Under the Deaconry of Doncaster, the 1595 List of Recusants gives:

SHEFFEELD. Roger HAYTON Joyner valet in bonis xli.
William RAWSON resydinge with his father James Rawson valet in bonis
        xli.
William FFRANKISHE Batchelor nil valet.
Francis STANIFORDE wedowe valet in bonis xxli.
Wenifride ELVISH wife of Raphe Elvishe valet in bonis xxli.
CLAYTON wife of Lurence Clayton valet in bonis vli.
John DUNN sonne of of Richard Dunn nil valet.
EGGLEFEELD cum BRADFEELD. Ellen GRAVES wedow residing in
        Wadslay nil valet.[1]

To these are added several names in a list of 1604:

SHEFFIELD PAROCH
William RAWSON, Roger HOWTON, William FRAUNKYSHE,
        Wenefrede, the wief of Rauf ELUYSHE, Nicholas
        CLAYTON, wief of Lawrence CLAYTON, Recusants for xii
        yeres: Lawrence CLAYTON, Non-Communicant at Easter.
James HOLLAND, William SAMPSON, Nicoles BEETE, Richard
        HORNER, Robert GESLYN, John BATLEY—
        Schoolmasters, and come not to ye Church.
BRADFIELD
OXLEY wedow, late wief of Edmund Oxley, hath sojourned there for one
        yeare or thereabouts, and came not to ye church, and yet she is
        now fled and gone—a Recusant.
Margaret, ye wief of Richard REVELL, of Stannington; Thomas
        REVELL there son, of xx yeres of age—Non-communicants at
        Easter last.
EAGLEFIELD
Hellene GREAVES, of Waddisley, in yt parish, wedow; Mary, her
        doghter—Recusants for many years.[2]

---

1. *CRS* 53, p. 16.
2. Edward Peacock, *A List of the Roman Catholics in the County of York in 1604* (London: Society of Antiquaries, 1872); reprinted in Hadfield, p. 7, together with Silkstone, Worsborough, Wath-upon-Dearne and Knaresborough.

Stannington and Spinkhill

No certain knowledge of a Mass centre in Sheffield has come down to us, but the Revell family of Nethergate Hall, Stannington certainly maintained one. As early as 1573, Avery Keller, a servant, was arrested while delivering a Mass book to the Revell house. The charge against Keller names John Revell, the scholars Palmer and Falconer, and Skinner the priest. Fortunately for the Revells, the matter ended there, and the family maintained an unbroken record of recusancy throughout penal times.

The Revells moved from Nethergate Hall to Revell Grange in 1742, and owing to the failure of the direct male line, the family continued there under the successive names of Broomhead, Wright and Sutton.[1]

Revell Grange was in continuous use as a Mass centre until 1828, when Mass was discontinued owing to the shortage of priests. The mission was reopened, however, in 1855.[2] The names and dates of priests who served at Stannington are not recorded, but Jesuits from Spinkhill and later seminary priests from Sheffield probably served the mission. There has been a Jesuit presence at Spinkhill since 1580, initially as chaplains to the Pole family. When the male line of the family died out in 1718, the Society redeemed the Spinkhill estate from another claimant. Up to that time, no fewer than nineteen Poles had become Jesuits, at least nine of them from Spinkhill.[3]

Catholic missions at Barlborough, Bolsterstone, Holbeck, Wingerworth and Winsley were served from Spinkhill.[4] One writer connects the Jesuits William Pennington and Robert Percy, who were at Spinkhill from 1701, with Stannington, but this is not confirmed elsewhere.[5] The earliest priest confidently connected with Sheffield is Fr Ignatius Brooke, SJ. But first it is necessary to review the changing climate of toleration in Sheffield.

1. Hadfield, pp. 12-13.
2. *CD*, 1856.
3. Information of Mr A. Havenhand.
4. Foley, vol. II, p. 273; vol. III, p. 135; vol. V, pp. 478-79, 512.
5. *Catholic Monthly* (July 1950).

Chapter 2

THE OLD CHAPEL

Sheffield in the Eighteenth Century

When Edward, the 8th Earl of Shrewsbury, died in 1617, there was no male heir of the Talbot line. Through his niece, Alethea, wife of Thomas, Earl of Arundel and Surrey, the vast Shrewsbury estates including Sheffield passed therefore into the possession of the House of Howard, a connection which continues to the present time.[1] Worksop Manor rather than Sheffield became the principal ducal seat. Following the Civil War, the castle at Sheffield was dismantled according to government policy. But the Manor House remained, and here successive ducal agents—Francis Ratcliffe, Arthur Palmer and John Shireburn—lived with their families and administered the Sheffield estates.

Following his accession in 1701, Duke Thomas, a Catholic, ordered the dismantling of the greater part of the Manor House.[2] He moved the agent to another house on the edge of the town, until a more suitable one could be built. John Shireburn's temporary dwelling was in Coal Pit Lane, which ran from Barker's Pool to The Moor, and is now called Cambridge Street. Attached to the house was the first post-Reformation Catholic chapel in Sheffield. John Shireburn was a kinsman of Fr William Pennington, SJ. It is probable, therefore, that Jesuits from Spinkhill served the Sheffield chapel.[3]

1. Mary Walton, *Sheffield, Its Story and Its Achievements* (Sheffield: The Sheffield Telegraph, 1952), p. 64.
2. Gatty, p. 93.
3. *Catholic Monthly* (July 1950); *CRS* 9, p. 182; *CRS* 70, p. 189.

The Lord's House

Eventually John Shireburn was to move his chapel to the new house situated in Fargate, at the corner of Norfolk Row. It had an elegant front, five bays wide and two storeys high, with a hipped roof. The central bays were stepped forward slightly and further accentuated by a triangular pediment. The central door had a semicircular pediment. The front was enclosed by a low segmental wall with a palisade. The garden stretched from the rear of the house, along Norfolk Row, as far as Norfolk Street.[1]

Plate 2 The Lord's House, Fargate, 1711

Throughout the eighteenth century, the house is referred to under various names in the accounts kept by successive ducal agents, for example, new intended building, new intended house, new building,

1. The engraving in Hunter, p. 284, looks plausible. That in Hadfield (facing p. 40) has the appearance of being drawn from memory by an amateur, since it bears several unlikely features.

new house, new house and office, the Accomptant's house, Norfolk Arms House, His Grace's house, Vincent Eyre's [the agent] house, Duke of Norfolk's House, The Duke's House occupied by Mr Eyre. Nowhere in the accounts is it called The Lord's House. Nevertheless that name will be used here, following Hadfield for the sake of clarity.

The agent John Shireburn came to Sheffield in December 1709. The accounts reveal that the Manor House was partly under demolition in October 1710, by which time Shireburn must have been at Coal Pit Lane. Plans were now afoot for The Lord's House. On 14th November, Shireburn paid

> Mr John Stanley, the Surveyor and Carpenter for drawing 2 or 3 designs at several times for the new intended House at Sheffield, £2. 3s. 0d.[1]

Subsequently Stanley was paid for making visits from his home at Holbeck Woodhouse, for work variously listed as consultations, contriving, directing, instructing, advising, and measuring. Stanley was the undoubted architect of The Lord's House, although the term architect was not then current. Occasionally, however, he did carpentry work on the house:

> 18 May 1711. Paid Mr Jno Stanley the Joyner for makeing two large Sash Windows, for the Great Staircase and office chamber on the back side of the new building, £4. 13s. 6d. 24 January 1713. For 6 pounds of Candles bought at several times for Mr Stanley ye Joyner working in ye night £0. 2s. 9d.[2]

John Shireburn the agent laid the foundation stone of the house on 19th March 1711, giving to the masons 4s. 6d 'according to Custome'. When the roof was finished, on 20th August 1711, the agent paid £4. 3s. 0d:

> For all the workmen and other assistance being a good number who according to Custome had their Suppers and plenty of Ale at Mr Ashmore's.

Finally, when the house was newly occupied, the agent records:

> Paid Mr Ashmore's Bill for His Grace's dinner at his house in Sheffield with my Lady Dutchess and Sir Nicholas Shireburn and His Lady, and at least one hundred Persons on ye 14 of July (1712) £20. 5s. $8\frac{1}{2}$.[3]

1. Arundel, S 169.
2. Arundel, S 169.
3. Arundel, S 169; S 160. The Duchess Maria was the daughter of Sir Nicholas and Lady Shireburn.

The Lord's House got away to a good beginning in its century of service.

The Old Chapel

In all of the accounts that refer to house, office and stable, there is no mention of the building of a chapel. This is not too surprising, considering the need for Catholics to be circumspect about their technically illegal worship. William Fairbank's plan, drawn in 1790 and reproduced by Hadfield, shows The Lord's House facing Fargate, behind it the office wing and the probable position of the Old Chapel, with its approach from Norfolk Row. This must have been one of the earliest Catholic chapels of the eighteenth century. As was customary with illicit chapels, the exterior was most likely given a domestic appearance in order not to attract unwelcome attention from hostile anti-Catholic factions.

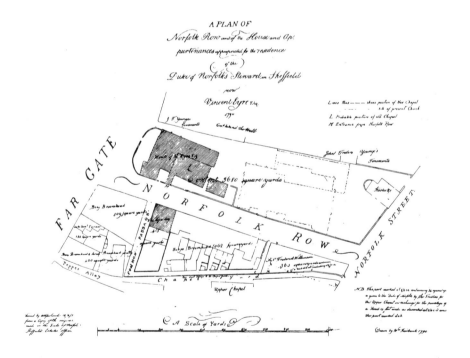

Plate 3 Plan of The Lord's House and the Old Rectory in 1790

The Old Chapel measured, according to Hadfield, about 50 ft by 28 ft inside, and with its gallery may have accommodated about 600 people. It was entered by a lobby or porch from Norfolk Row. At the end nearer Fargate (opposite the altar) was a gallery reached by stairs, in which was the Duke of Norfolk's pew, which could also be approached from the house through an ante-room used as a vestry. John Shireburn and several successive agents lived in The Lord's House, and conducted the Duke's affairs in the adjacent office. Thomas, the 8th Duke lived at Worksop Manor.

Father Ignatius Brooke

Active in the Sheffield district during these years was a Jesuit priest, Fr Ignatius Brooke. A native of Maryland, born in 1671, he came to Europe, was ordained at Valladolid (1696), joined the Society of Jesus (1699), and served at Valladolid and at Watten in Flanders. He came to England in 1711 and worked in the Midlands from the College of the Immaculate Conception at Spinkhill. He was rector there from 1728 to 1735 and is recorded as serving at Bolsterstone and Stannington c. 1724-33.[1]

Fr Brooke probably served Sheffield regularly from 1711, but it would be misleading to assume that he was resident there. It is more likely that he resided at Spinkhill and travelled on horseback to Sheffield and other Mass centres. He is recorded as chaplain when Bishop Williams, making his Visitation in July 1728, confirmed 62 persons in Sheffield (at the Duke of Norfolk's chapel), and 23 persons perhaps at Stannington or Bolsterstone.[2] Fr Brooke probably left the Midlands by 1735, and died at St Omer's in 1751.

Duke Thomas died in 1732 and was succeeded by his brother Edward, 9th Duke. It has been suggested that Duke Edward was averse to Jesuits and that this was why Fr Brooke left the Sheffield mission. At all events, a Seminary priest, Fr Edward Matthews, was at Sheffield from 1733 until 1734, and Fr Thomas Holdford (alias Hunt) in 1735. A Jesuit, James Fox (alias Poole or Pole), continued at

---

1. The various notes on Ignatius Brooke in Foley, vol. V, p. 708; vol. VII, p. 90; and *CRS* 13, p. 178; 25, p. 112; and 30, p. 178 tend to conflict. This account follows the recent note of Fr Geoffrey Holt SJ in *CRS* 70, pp. 42-43.

2. *CRS* 25, p. 112.

Bolsterstone to 1739, and John Boarman was there in 1769.[1] We have no record of independent priestly provision for Stannington from then on. Possibly the mission was served from Sheffield, but documentary evidence is lacking.

William Statham

In tracing the history of Sheffield Catholics in times of repression, we are constantly hampered by the dearth of primary sources of information. The movements of priests may be plotted, and the financial papers of the ducal estate have revealed the building history of The Lord's House. At this point we are also fortunate in being able to refer to the extant diary of a Catholic layman. William Statham (1694–1734) kept his diary in adult life, but happily also recorded the facts of his origins and childhood. As a young man he experienced conversion to the Catholic faith, and among the journalistic entries are many pages of prayers and devotional thoughts. The volume also contains the writer's will and final letters to his wife and daughter. It is as valuable for its rarity as for its contents. The following lines attempt to portray William Statham as a Sheffield Catholic.[2]

William Statham was born at Tideswell in 1694, the sixth child of a 'practitioner in law', as he expressed it. His schooling was spasmodic, owing to his poor health, but he visited Sheffield at the age of nine to be taught reading by Mrs Bingley, 'an instructor of children . . . at the sign of the Rose and Crown entry'. At the age of twelve he attended the school of a Mrs Sitwell in Church Lane. Later still he went to school 'to learn writing and arithmetic' from the teacher Samuel Moor. At the age of sixteen he was sent to Hull to become acquainted with navigation and arithmetic, and this led to his apprenticeship to William Poyntz, a Portugal merchant. He stayed four days in London where he saw the lions, the Tower, St Paul's Cathedral and the Monument, then travelled to Falmouth to set sail for Portugal. He worked in Lisbon for several years with Poyntz, who dealt in woollen goods.

1. *Catholic Monthly* (July 1950); Anstruther, vol. IV, pp. 141, 188; Foley, vol. V, p. 708; *CRS* 32, p. 309; *CRS* 70, pp. 36, 96.
2. I have referred to Michael Field, 'Life in Sheffield 300 Years Ago', in *The Star* (25 Nov. 1980), as well as to the diary held at Sheffield City Library under classification MD 6853 (a).

At the age of 23, Statham came home and married a local girl, Frances Shirecliff, in Ecclesfield church. After a short time he returned to Portugal, leaving Frances with his mother. Following news of the birth of a daughter, Mary, he came home. Finding his wife 'pale and weakly', he determined to remain with his family. In 1720 Statham purchased a small estate at Shiregreen from Joshua Fox for £375, where he grew crops and acquired cattle, a mare and some chickens. As well as his wife and daughter, his mother lived with him, and also his sister Frances who later married Mr Hunt, a mercer of Sheffield.

About this time Statham records that he left off frequenting the Church of England. Not long after moving to his new home, he began to attend the Catholic chapel, and refers to Fr Ignatius Brooke as his spiritual father. He was received into the Catholic Church on 4 December 1720. His nearest Catholic chapel was that at Sheffield, and he records taking his daughter there on St George's day in 1724. Later, he proudly records, 'I was confirmed at Sheffield in the Duke of Norfolk's chapel by the name of Thomas' on Sunday 14th July 1728.

In 1725 Statham relates how he assisted the ducal agent:

> In the beginning of my 31st year John Shireburn esq. of Sheffield, chief steward to his Grace the Duke of Norfolk sent to me to come and assist him in the Duke's affairs as Clark. I thinking my handwriting not sufficient I went to my old writing master Samuel Moor to learn Secretary and entered March 25 into the service of Thomas, Duke of Norfolk.

> In September John Shireburn esq. brisk and cheerful went to attend his Grace Thomas Duke of Norfolk at Worksop Manor so I attended my Old Master and was his assistant in passing his accounts as Chief Steward, giving our great and gracious Master a full relation of all his rents and affairs appertaining to all his several estates in this Kingdom, of Arundel, London, Stonyhurst, Sheffield, Worksop and Norfolk.

Owing to anti-Catholic disturbances in 1723, when he was arrested and his house was searched for arms, Statham decided to leave his Shiregreen estate. He took a small house with some land at £5 per annum at The Hill in Derbyshire. Here he generally attended the chapel at Thorp, the house of Thomas Eyre, but suggests also that he joined in Catholic worship in Hathersage.

William Statham's diary is followed by his will, dated December 1734, leaving his goods and money to his wife and daughter, and a legacy to the poor of Norton parish. In a moving letter to his daughter, he desired her to be governed by the Duke of Norfolk's steward, whom he made one of his executors. In conclusion, he directs that stipends be paid to Fr Ignatius Brooke and to the altars at Sheffield and Hathersage, 'that the Holy Sacrifice of the Church may be offered up by the faithful for my sinful soul'. William Statham died shortly after making his will.

The Visitation Return of 1735

William Statham's name appears on the list of Sheffield Catholics made in 1735. John Dossie, the Vicar of Sheffield, supplied this list, or Visitation Return, to Lancelot Blackburn, Archbishop of York. Dossie seems ignorant, however, of Bishop Williams's visit to Sheffield and the Confirmation there in 1728. Since many of the names still have a clear Sheffield ring about them, the Return is reproduced here in full.

> Sheffield–Doncaster
> Septmb. 17: 1735
> Sir. In obedience to His Grace the Lord Archbishop of York's comands I now send you a list of the names of all Papists, or Supposed, with their Titles, Distinctions, or Trades.
> Mr Benjamin BLACKBURN, steward to the Duke of Norfolk.
> John SMITHER, Margaret PARKER, and Elizabeth WILDSMITH his servants.
> Henry BROWNILL, Baker, and Anne his wife.
> Joseph FERNALLY, Labourer, and Martha his wife.
> John BROOMHEAD, Mercer, and 4 daughters, viz. Katherine, Jane, Elizabeth and Harriot.
> Thomas EYRE, Inn-Keeper, Richard CASE, Joiner.
> Henry BARKER, Blacksmith, and John BAYES his servt.
> Mark FURNISS, Wheelwright, and Anne his wife.
> George EYRE, comb-maker, and Rose his wife.
> John HAWKESWORTHE, Shoemaker, and Mary his wife.
> John HANCOCK, cutler, and Dorothy his wife.
> Gylford SYKES, cutler, and Mary his wife, and Phineas and Gylford, his sons, and Christian his daughter.
> George CHESHIRE, Cutler, and Elizabeth his wife.
> John MABLEY, file-smith, and Martha his wife.
> Matthew TRANFIELD, Cooper.
> Wm HOBSON, labourer, and Jane his wife.
> Phillip SMILBER, Woodward to the Duke of Norfolk.

Wm RYDIN, labourer, and Sarah his wife.
John EYRE, Collier, and Hannah his wife.
Robert FURNISS, Cutler, Elizabeth his wife, and Wm FURNISS his son.
Robert EYRE, Butcher, and Anne his sister.
Jonathan WEBSTER, Cutler, and Eliz: his wife.
Thomas HYDES, Button-maker.
Thomas PADLEY, Button-maker.
Richard WESTON, Button-maker.
William STATHAM, Farmer, and Anne, his daughter.
Thomas PARKER, Scissars-Smith.
Timothy PALFRIMAN, Cutler.
Thomas PALFRIMAN, Butcher.
John PALFRIMAN, Tailor.
John BROWNILL, Cutler, and Elizabeth his wife.
William FOSTER, Cutler, and Anne his wife.
George HALLAS, Collier.
Marmaduke HOLMES, labourer.
Mary MILNES, Widow.
Alice HARGRAVE, Widow.
Martha DYLAY, Widow.
Elizabeth DAMS, Widow.
William SORESBY, Malster, and Alice his wife.
Thomas WINDLE, Cutler, and Winifrid his wife.
Robert MARSHALL, Gardiner, and Helen his wife.
Phillip HUNTER, Husbandman.
Uriah CHOW, Husbandman.
Wm SAVAGE, Cutler, and Elizabeth his wife, Thomas BORE and
Bridget SMITH, his servants.
Wm CASTLETON, Husbandman.
Martha, the wife of Joshua SPOONER.

There is a person called Mr HUNT[1] who is suspected to be a popish
Priest, he lives with Mr Blackburn mentioned before, and at whose house
Mass is understood to be perform'd, and to wch there is a resort of
papists every Lord's day, or however very frequently.

I never heard yt there either is, or ever hath been any popish school for
persons of either sex in the parish of Sheffield, nor any Visitation, or
Confirmation held by any Popish Bishop there. WINDLE, and
BARKER, and FURNISS, and HANCOCK, and TRANFIELD, and
HYDES, PADLEY and WATSON [Weston?], and John BROWNILL
were formerly Protestants, but I cannot learn when, or by whom, they
were perverted.

1. Hunt was the alias of Fr Thomas Holdford: Anstruther, vol. IV, p. 141.

This Acct. of the number of Papists, is, according to the best information I can gett, a true one. It is possible in a parish so large and populous, as that of Sheffield is known to be, for some, yt are papists to escape the notice of the strictest enquirer, but I am perswaded, yt few, if any more, are to be found here, besides those, whose names are sett down in this paper.

I am, Sir,

Yo. Humble Serv.,

John Dossie.[1]

In the eighteenth century, it seems that Sheffield Catholics were a small but growing body, composed chiefly of artisans, and relying for their priests and chapel on the goodwill and beneficence of the Duke of Norfolk. There was considerable clerical stability, moreover, with only three priests successively in charge of the mission between 1736 and 1828.

1. *CRS* 32, pp. 308-309; E.S. Worrall, *Return of Papists 1767*, vol. II, pp. 48-49.

Chapter 3

THE NEW CHAPEL

Priests, 1736–1828

When in 1736 Fr Thomas Holdford (alias Hunt) left Sheffield to become chaplain to the Carryll family, he was succeeded by Fr Thomas Gradwell, a Douay priest. Fr Gradwell spent all his priestly life in Sheffield, dying there in 1758. He is described as 'a plain, sensible and pious man, a ripe scholar, and held in much esteem by all the people'.[1] During his twenty-two years in Sheffield, Fr Gradwell continued serving Stannington, and added to his list of cures that of Rotherham, where he said Mass once a month.[2]

Early in 1758, Fr John Lodge appears in the ducal agent's accounts as Fr Gradwell's paid assistant. Also, Fr Thomas Shimmell and Fr Charles Cordell are granted travelling expenses, while assisting at Sheffield during Fr Gradwell's last illness. Following Fr Gradwell's death, Fr Lodge continues alone as priest in charge.[3]

A Douay priest and a Yorkshireman, Fr Lodge was not of robust health and had a number of assistants, among them Fr William Winter (1764–75); and two natives of Sheffield, Fr Rowland Broomhead (1776–78) and Fr Samuel Sayles (1782–87).

In 1786 Fr Lodge moved to Durham, where he died in 1795.[4] In his place came Fr Richard Rimmer, a Douay priest, born in Lancashire, an amiable man who impressed his compatriots by his quiet application to the daily round of duty. He built the New Chapel in 1816, and died suddenly in 1828, having been missioner at Sheffield for over forty years.[5]

1. Hadfield, p. 22; Anstruther, vol. IV, p. 115.
2. *Catholic Monthly* (July 1950).
3. Arundel, S 165.
4. Anstruther, vol. IV, pp. 48, 175, 235, 306.
5. Anstruther, vol. IV, p. 229; *Catholic Monthly* (July 1950).

Ducal Agents

A succession of staunch Catholic Dukes of Norfolk, and the presence in Sheffield of their agents or stewards, assisted this vigorous mission, especially through the generous provision of the chapel and of salaried priests. John Shireburn's reign as agent seems to have lasted from 1709 to 1726. His successor was Benjamin Blackburn, who died in 1736. Blackburn was named in the Recusant Return of 1735, and maintained a domestic chapel at Bolsterstone.[1] Vincent Eyre (the first of two of that name) followed Blackburn as agent in 1736, dying in 1761. He is recorded as maintaining a domestic chapel at Highfield in Chesterfield, and went to live there in 1756.[2] In 1761 Duke Edward made his kinsman Henry Howard agent in Sheffield, where several sons were born, including Bernard Edward, destined to become the 12th Duke in 1815.

The second Vincent Eyre was in the Duke's service at London and Sheffield in 1773, and was successor to Henry Howard as Sheffield agent from 1776 to his death in 1801. He was responsible for the development of Alsop Fields, which lay between Norfolk Street and the River Sheaf, and for naming the new streets after himself and members of the House of Howard. Also in the office at this time were George Townsend (1784–90), John Barnard (1790–95) and Michael Johnson (1795–1812).[3] Vincent Henry Eyre succeeded his father and resigned in 1813. He was followed by John Housman, who died in 1819. Then two Michael Ellisons, father and son, agents successively to the 12th, 13th, 14th and 15th Dukes, take this catalogue beyond the scope of this chapter.[4]

1. Foley, vol. VII, p. 90; *CRS* 13, p. 178; *CRS* 32, p. 308.

2. Ralph Baines SJ, 'Manuscript History of Spinkhill', pp. 253 and 276, at Archives of the English Province; Hunter, p. 158.

3. Arundel, S 173 (14 and 15 Sept. 1773); Gillow, vol. II, p. 204.

4. Information of Dr J.M. Robinson, Librarian to the Duke of Norfolk; *Catalogue of the Arundel Castle Manuscripts* (Sheffield: Libraries and Arts Committee, 1965), pp. 27-28. The names and dates of earlier and later agents may be gleaned from the Catalogue.

The Old Chapel: Finance

Small details emerge from the ducal stewards' accounts, happily preserved among the Arundel Castle Manuscripts. Occasional supplies of linen and candles appear: two gowns, one for Worksop Manor, the other for Sheffield, £1. 4s. 0d; a quantity of Holland for the altar, 6s. 6d (1736); candlesticks for the chapel, £2. 14s. 0d (1760); Mr Wildsmith for a carpet for the chapel altar, £1. 12s. 6d (1772). Mr Vennor supplied linen for the chapel, Mr Didsbury supplied silk and Mrs Betty Martin was paid for sewing and lining work (1776). There was plastering, painting and repair work done to the fabric of the chapel in 1740; Charles Wharton for whitewashing the chapel was paid £1. 6s. 0d and Mr Fenton for painting the chapel windows, shutters etc., £4. 3s. $3\frac{1}{2}$d (1777).

The salaries of the chaplains were paid half-yearly. Fr Gradwell received £30 per annum; his successors Fr Lodge and Fr Rimmer £42. 10s. The chaplain was also awarded £20 per annum to distribute to the poor. From 1783 Fr Samuel Sayles as assistant to Fr Lodge received a £20 salary which specifically included his allowance for the upkeep of a horse, no doubt to travel to Stannington, Rotherham and elsewhere.[1]

Darnall Hall

When Henry Howard became agent, he held nominal occupation of The Lord's House, but he also rented another house, Darnall Hall, at £70 per annum. From at least 1773 Henry Howard had his own chaplains at Darnall, independent of those at The Lord's House. Fr Thomas Hayes SJ died at Darnall Hall, probably in 1774.[2]

Fr John Eyre served next at Darnall, but was compelled by ill health to retire eventually to The Farm in Sheffield, where he died in 1790. (He was the brother of the Duke's agent Vincent Eyre; of Fr Edward Eyre, who was rector at Hathersage from 1795 to 1834; and of Fr Thomas Eyre, President of Ushaw College in 1808–10)[3]. Fr Eyre's place at Darnall Hall was taken by another Douay priest, Fr

1. Arundel, S 165, S 173.
2. Arundel, S 165 (Midsummer 1763); *CRS* 70, p. 115; Foley, vol. VII, p. 349.
3. Anstruther, vol. IV, pp. 98-100; Gillow, vol. II, pp. 202-203.

William Fletcher, from about 1777. He disappears from the records following the demise of Henry Howard in 1787, when the chaplaincy was probably discontinued. Only Fr Fletcher's death is noted, at Sunderland in 1812.[1]

Catholics and the Law

Despite the penal laws, which banned priests and assemblies of Catholics, barred the inheritance or purchase of land, and yet imposed a double land tax, Catholics contrived to survive in eighteenth-century England. They did so largely owing to the patronage of the titled and the wealthy gentry. Their upkeep of domestic chapels and their maintenance of priests enabled the rank and file to adhere to the practice of their faith. The Sheffield experience of ducal patronage was part of a pattern repeated in many places in the land. Catholics wisely held a low profile, and for the most part were not so much persecuted as simply ignored. Thus the Yorkshire Catholic gentry held aloof from the Stuart risings of 1715 and 1745 and thereby avoided reprisals. The agent's accounts record damage to the parish church in 1718, but there are no anti-Catholic overtones:

> Repairing and upholstering the seats, and glass windows at Sheffield Church Chancel, quarter ending Michaelmas last, and for other repairs of glass broke in the night by the Mobb. £0. 14s. 5d.[2]

The only example discovered of persecution is that experienced by the Catholic diarist William Statham. When he was living at Shiregreen in 1723, Statham writes of an alleged national plot exposed by an anti-Catholic faction. It mainly concerned the lawyer Christopher Layer, a confirmed Jacobite conspirator, but also involved was Dr Francis Atterbury, Bishop of Rochester, who leant towards Jacobitism.[3] The outcome of the alarm was the banishment of Dr Atterbury and the execution of Christopher Layer. It was then followed by

> A general search in the houses of all Papists for Armes; and all persons to swear allegiance or else be reputed Enemys of the State. I was brought in amongst them, my house searched, and a value of my lands given in,

1. Anstruther, vol. IV, p. 104; Hadfield, pp. 25-26.
2. Arundel, S 170 (11 March 1718).
3. On Atterbury and Layer, see *DNB*, vol. II, p. 233, and vol. XXXII, p. 304.

which put me upon a Resolution of selling my Estate again (for I had none to assist me; everyone stood afar off either imagining I should be frightened to relinquish the Catholic Faith or else no body had any regard for me, except my sister Mary Statham who vindicated me against the Men as much as could be expected).[1]

As a result of this incident, William Statham sold his Shiregreen farm to Robert Ellis 'a Derbyshire Man' for £295, and moved to the neighbourhood of Hathersage. Generally, however, it was a time of live and let live. While listing 82 suspected Papists for the Visitation Return, John Dossie, the Vicar of Sheffield, indicated his own uncertainty over the presence of a resident priest, or the frequency of Mass, or the occurrence of episcopal Visitation or Confirmation. Clearly, Catholics were reasonably safe from persecution in Sheffield, but took pains not to draw attention to themselves or to their chapel.

Following the 9th Duke's scheme initiated in 1774 of transporting coal to the town by means of an early type of railway, there was prolonged unrest owing to the groundless suspicion that this would increase the price of coal. Serious riots broke out in which trucks, rails and buildings were damaged or destroyed. The agent's accounts record a payment:

15 May 1776. Bate Hatter and Neighbour who informed the Family of the rioters coming in the night to Demolish the Duke's House. £0. 5s. 0d.[2]

The house was not demolished in the riots, and the threat to it was economic rather than anti-Catholic in origin. Its windows were afterwards fortified, but without any urgency:

7 Jan. 1777. William Gray, Blacksmith, for an Iron frame for ye Staircase Window of His Grace's house at Sheffield and also for window bars for said house. £5. 13s. 0d.

23 June 1778. Thos. Darwin, Whitesmith, for an Iron frame for the outside of Mr Howard's Office Window. £2. 19s. 0d.[3]

Probably more alarming was the news that came from London in June 1780. A mild measure of toleration two years earlier had repealed the penalty of life imprisonment for Catholic bishops, priests

1. Diary of William Statham, (1723), pp. 98-99.
2. Arundel S 173; R.E. Leader, *Sheffield in the Eighteenth Century* (Sheffield: The Sheffield Independent Press, 1905), pp. 84-85.
3. Arundel, S 173.

and schoolmasters. This provoked the formation of the Protestant Association under the leadership of the eccentric Lord George Gordon. The Association's demands for the repeal of the Act led to a week of uncontrollable riots in London, during which the houses and chapels of Catholics were destroyed.[1]

Repercussions in the provinces were limited to Bath, where the chapel, house and archives of Bishop Walmsley were burnt. At Sheffield no disturbance apparently occurred. The agent merely records:

> 15 June 1780. By several Persons to Guard the House from the Mob apprehended to rise—£0. 15s. 0d.[2]

Building Matters, 1779

About this time there are references in the accounts to a 'New Building':

> 23 June 1779. Abraham Birtles, mason, New Building at Sheffield House. £1. 13s. 4d.
> 8 Oct. 1779. Henry Browne, Carpenter, work done at the new building adjacent to the House. £31. 10s. 0d.

Various payments continue for masonry, plasterwork, carpentry, ironwork and slates, until finally:

> 15 April 1780. Samuel Walker, Six Chimney Tops for the additional building for the Sheffield house. £1. 11s. 6d.[3]

Probably the clergy house is meant, on the opposite side of Norfolk Row from The Lord's House. This is marked on Fairbank's plan of 1790 as reproduced by Hadfield. It was noted as occupied by Fr Rimmer in a deed of 1824 and may well have been designated for the clergy from its inception in 1779.[4] It still stands, as numbers 4–6 Norfolk Row. In a room here, the forerunner of St Marie's School was founded by Fr George Keasley about 1830–35.

---

1. On the Gordon Riots, see C. Hibbert, *King Mob* (London: Longmans, Green, 1958).

2. Arundel, S 185 no. 3; Brian Plumb, *Arundel to Zabi* (Warrington: Brian Plumb, 1988), unpaged; see under Walmsley.

3. Arundel, S 173.

4. Hadfield, p. 35 and facing p. 38.

Fr Pratt and his assistant Fr Kavanagh are recorded as living there. Soon after Fr Scully's arrival in 1850, he moved with his assistant Fr Joseph Hill to the house at the corner of Norfolk Row and Norfolk Street formerly occupied by Sir Arnold Knight. This house (which also still stands) served the clergy until the present rectory was completed in 1904.[1] Fr Rimmer continued to receive his personal allowance, now £100, and £10 for the poor. The Duke also subscribed five guineas per annum to the Sheffield Catholic Sunday School.

Plate 4 The Old Rectory in Norfolk Row, 1780

Vincent Eyre, the agent to the Duke, died in 1801, and was succeeded by his son. Vincent Henry Eyre resigned in 1813, and was succeeded by John Housman. The Lord's House was vacated and the accounts now record the occupation of land, house and offices at The Farm. John Housman died in 1819, after which in addition to The Farm, the agency had offices and a house in Eyre Street occupied by the agent Michael Ellison.[2]

1. Hadfield, pp. 67, 75, 77, 121.
2. Arundel, S 166, S 167.

The New Chapel

In 1814 The Lord's House was dismantled and the ground sold to a syndicate of Catholic gentlemen. Part of it was conveyed to Fr Rimmer, who had the New Chapel built, with a graveyard fronting Norfolk Row. The Old Chapel of The Lord's House was not pulled down until the New Chapel was ready, this being opened on 1st May 1816, having cost about £3,000. The New Chapel stood at the northeast corner of the present cathedral, approximately upon the parts now occupied by the Blessed Sacrament chapel, the north transept, the Mortuary chapel, the north aisle, and a narrow space outside these, to the north and east. It was of rectangular plan with six tall round-headed windows at the sides, and had an organ gallery at the west end. Approximately 85 ft by 40 ft, it was substantially larger than the Old Chapel.

Plate 5 The New Chapel, 1816–1847

Fr Rimmer laboured in the New Chapel for twelve years until his sudden death on 12 May 1828. He had been priest of the Sheffield mission for over forty years, and was characterized by the Derbyshire poet Richard Furniss in lines that ended:

A good Samaritan he was, and sought out need;
Came where it was, and gave, and bless'd indeed.[1]

The accounts about this time contain two puzzling entries:

29 November 1817, to Mr Woolhouse for work done at the new chapel.
£5. 13s. 8d;
3 August 1819 to John Rawstorne the architect for Plans etcetera.
£2. 2s. 0d.

Henry Woolhouse and Sons of Broad Street may well have been the builders of the chapel. No corroborating evidence has been found, however, to attribute its design to John Rawstorne.[2]

Priests, 1828 to 1843

Fr Andrew Macartney, assistant since 1826, became rector following the death of Fr Rimmer. He had as assistants Fr George Heptonstall (1828–29) and Fr Michael Bimson (1829–30). Following the departure of Fr Macartney, long-term stability was restored with the rectorship of Fr George Keasley from 1830 to 1839. He had as assistants Fr Robert Tate (1830–32), Fr Thomas Fisher (1833–36), Fr Charles Brigham (1836–37), and Fr Joseph Kerr (1837–39). Then Fr James Sharples, later to be coadjutor Vicar Apostolic of the Lancashire District, was rector during the years 1839–43. His assistants were Fr Thomas Holden (1839-43) and Fr Marcus Supple (1840–42).[3]

Only Fr George Keasley need detain us. He was responsible for the erection of the parish schools in Surrey Street in 1835–36, at a cost of £1,800. These were superseded by the new girls' and boys' schools of 1858 and 1878. After a very chequered career, the school building became the Registry Office, and was demolished in 1974, following the opening of a new office nearby.[4]

Fr Keasley was also responsible for the enlargement of the chapel. The installation of a new organ (by J.C. Bishop at an outlay of £900) required a much larger gallery, and as the body of the chapel was

1. Hadfield, pp. 32-42.
2. Arundel, S 166, S 167.
3. *Laity's Directory* to 1837; *CD* from 1838. Besides these names the registers yield: John Rigby, J. Harrison, J. Canut, Hugh Quigley, Matthew Henry Smith. See Hadfield, pp. 62, 80.
4. *Catholic Monthly* (July 1950); Hadfield, p. 51.

rather small for the number of regular worshippers, the opportunity was taken to extend the building by adding a new bay to the west, with a gallery sufficiently large to take the new organ. The extension comprised a Doric portico and extra congregational space at ground level, with stairs leading to the upper floor. This contained a passage leading to a private room, as well as the organ and space for the choir.[1]

Plate 6 The Surrey Street School, 1833–1878

1. Hadfield, pp. 51-53; Sheffield City Library, seven plans of the Catholic Chapel (1838), AP 55.

Chapter 4

THE FIRST CHURCH:
ST MARIE

Fr Charles Pratt

Fr Pratt became senior priest in Sheffield, in succession to Fr Sharples, in 1843. A young man of great energy, he initiated a chancel choir and the first post-Reformation mission in Sheffield, given by two Rosminian Fathers. One of them, Dr Luigi Gentili, advocated greater devotion to Our Lady and the setting up of her statue. A statue was afterwards installed in the New Chapel, and moved eventually to a niche over the north door of St Marie's church.

Above all, Fr Pratt saw the need for a much larger church. To this end he first acquired extra land to the west of the chapel; then he enlisted the service of Mr Hadfield, an architect and a member of his congregation.

Matthew Hadfield

Matthew Hadfield was the nephew of Michael Ellison, agent to the Duke of Norfolk's Sheffield estates. Following articles with Messrs Woodhead and Hurst of Doncaster, and London experience with Peter Robinson, Hadfield began to practise in Sheffield. From 1838, he was in partnership with John Gray Weightman. Since Weightman was an Anglican and Hadfield was a Catholic, the firm obtained work from both denominations, to the number of some thirty churches, between 1838 and 1850.

In the aftermath of the Napoleonic Wars, when little building had taken place, and in the light of immigration and the Catholic Revival, many new churches were required.[1] Gothic Revival was the generally

1. Welsh.

preferred style, and this experienced its finest flowering in the decade 1840 to 1850. Owing to the pioneering work of the Camden Society and the theory and practice of the Catholic architect A.W.N. Pugin, the quality of design in church art and architecture improved immeasurably. Previous uninformed attempts at Gothic copyism now gave way to scholarly recreations of mediaeval examples.

Plate 7 St Andrew's Church, Heckington

It was fortunate for Sheffield that Matthew Hadfield came under the influence of Pugin. With such admirable Catholic churches as those at Rotherham and Salford already to his credit, Hadfield possessed the expertise required to fulfil Sheffield's needs. Hadfield had studied carefully such prime examples of Decorated Gothic as the churches of Howden and Beverley. Moreover, during the year 1847, he and Fr Pratt visited Lincoln Cathedral and the churches of Newark, Sleaford, Ewerby and Heckington. In the event, the design of St Marie's was based upon a close study of the fourteenth-century St Andrew's at Heckington.[1]

Building Matters, 1847

Having acquired land for his new church, Fr Pratt negotiated for the use of Mount Tabor Chapel at the corner of Rockingham Street and Wellington Street. This was blessed by Bishop Briggs on 16th January 1847. It was to serve as a temporary church for over three years. The New Chapel was demolished; certain necessary disinterments took place, and the remains were reburied. Building operations on the church began, and Bishop Briggs blessed the foundation stone on 25th March.

Sadly, Fr Pratt died on 17th February 1849, before the church was complete. As there was no Catholic burial ground in Sheffield, he was interred at St Bede's, Rotherham. Just over a year later, his remains were brought back secretly, and reinterred in the tomb which the builder Benjamin Gregory had prepared on the north side of the chancel.

Fr Pratt's place was taken for about a year by Fr William Parsons. Then Fr Edmund Scully became rector, and he it was who guided building and furnishing matters to a triumphant conclusion, culminating in the opening of the church.[2]

St Marie's Cathedral Church

Hemmed in on three sides by various buildings, the exterior of St Marie's Cathedral Church is not easily viewed. But from the south-east at least, the ensemble of church, sacristies and rectory presents a composition of great charm. The view of the church in particular, with its tower, porch, Lady chapel, east window and numerous gables, offers a variety of emphases to the eye. Writing on the Gothic Revival, the Victorian scholar Charles Eastlake observed:

1. Hadfield, pp. 73, 75.
2. Hadfield, pp. 67-69, 77-81.

The masonry of this and other churches erected by Mr Hadfield exhibits evidence of an appreciation of those 'true principles' of constructive detail which were then more preached than practised.

The window arches etc. instead of being turned in large blocks of stone, according to the prevailing custom, are executed in small and numerous voussoirs, which give scale and significance to the work. The wall courses, instead of being rubbed down to the smoothness of paper (a method of finish at once wasteful of labour and uninteresting in effect) are left simply dressed with the chisel. The mouldings are delicately and sharply cut, and the details of ironwork in the screens etc., are handled with a vigour far in advance of the time.[1]

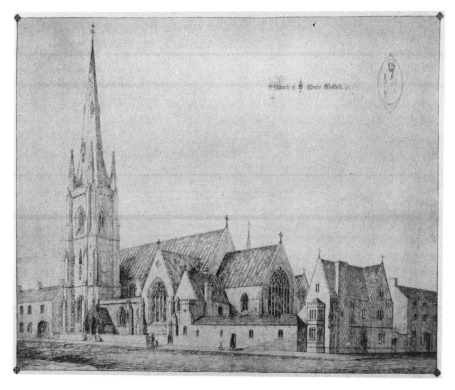

Plate 8 St Marie's Church in 1850

The architect afforded the sculptor ample opportunity to exhibit his skill. Particularly striking are the niches and crocketed gables that

1. C. Eastlake, *A History of The Gothic Revival* (London: Longmans, Green, 1872), p. 243.

decorate the lower stages of the tower, nave and porch, and the numerous stone heads that flank the windows.

The interior is a perfect model of fourteenth-century design, interpreted in those Gothic Revival terms current in the 1840s, and subsequently beautified with numerous permanent furnishings. The plan consists of nave with south-west tower, aisles, transepts, a deep chancel, three east chapels, a chapel off the north aisle and a south porch. The nave is of six bays, with clerestory and wagon roof. Its piers (after Heckington) are of square plan, with demi-columns at each face and plain moulded capitals. Structural additions since 1850 have been few and tasteful. They concern the Lady chapel and several new windows. To give extra natural light to the interior, the west window of the south transept was cut out of the wall in 1874 by the builder John Pearson, the firm of Hadfield being the supervising architects. At the same time, a similar window was cut in the corresponding place in the north transept wall abutting the Mortuary chapel. The cost of the work was donated by the Duke of Norfolk.[1]

In 1889, additional windows were cut in the clerestory, four on the south side and three on the north. The architect, Charles Hadfield, made a slight distinction here, designing quatrefoils in the tracery of the new work in contrast with trefoils in the old. The contractor for this was George Webster of Intake Road.[2] Meanwhile in 1878–79, the new Lady chapel had been added to the church. The upper space in the south transept was originally an organ loft. The organ was moved to a west gallery in 1861. When the present organ was installed in the chancel in 1875, the old Bishop organ was sold and the west gallery was dismantled. This released the south transept gallery for adaptation as the Lady chapel.

Messrs Hadfield and Son produced a most attractive design, which included a projecting staircase and openwork balustrade. The chapel is dominated by the tall octagon with its rib vault raised over the altar. This and the supporting columns are set off by lush decoration of blank arcades with diaper infill and crocketed gables. The builder was John Pearson of Hanover Street; the marble altar was by Boulton, and other sculpture by Thomas Earp.[3]

1. Hadfield, pp. 158-59; Arundel, D 85.
2. *BN* (5 Apr. 1889), p. 497.
3. Hadfield, pp. 165-67.

St Marie's structural work apart, we must now survey the stained glass and other permanent furnishings.

Stained Glass Windows

St Marie's is rich in stained glass. When the church was opened in 1850, there were already several windows installed by Wailes of

Plate 9 Interior of St Marie's Church c. 1920

Newcastle. These included the great east window (designed by George Goldie), the window over the north door (Bulmer), the south transept south window (Wright), two windows in the south aisle (Fr Parsons, Frith family), three in the Blessed Sacrament chapel and three in the Mortuary chapel.[1] Two windows in the Blessed Sacrament chapel were renewed in 1988 by Messrs Goddard and Gibbs. By John Hardman of Birmingham are the great west window (1850, designed

1. Hadfield, p. 98.

by Pugin), the north transept window (1862, Michael Ellison), three windows in the Lady chapel octagon (1879), one in the south aisle (Cadman family †1859), and that in the baptistery to Canon Dolan, †1935.[1] By Lavers, Barraud, and Westlake are two windows on the staircase of the Lady chapel (designed by J.F. Bentley) and two in the Norfolk chantry.[2]

The 'Children' window in the west wall of the north aisle, donated in 1901 by Mr and Mrs Bernasconi, is signed by Mayer, the ecclesiastical furnishing suppliers of Munich and London. The Guardian Angels window in the north aisle was designed in 1889 by Atkinson of Newcastle.[3] Most recent is the window in the south transept commemorating the erection of Hallam Diocese in 1980, designed by Patrick Reyntiens. As yet undiscovered are the artists of the following: the English Martyrs window in the north aisle (to Canon Walshaw †1896), and the window beneath the tower (to John and Lavinia Bernasconi †1924).

Furnishings of 1850

Other noteworthy art work in 1850 included the following: the reredos, the original high altar, the effigy of Fr Pratt and the Lady statue above the north door, which came from the Lambeth workshop of John Myers. The reredos was designed by Pugin and sculptured by Theodore Phyffers; and Thomas Earp sculptured the effigy. Other stone sculpture was the work of Charles James, viz. the Blessed Sacrament altar, the chancel sedilia, the font, several foliage capitals and numerous head stops to arches, both inside and out.

Floor tiles for the chancel, the Blessed Sacrament chapel, and the Norfolk chantry were designed and supplied by Minton and Company of Stoke on Trent. Wood carving of the figures in the rood, the chancel stalls, ten angels in the chancel roof, and later the pulpit was by Arthur Hayball of Sheffield. Other carpentry work was done by Thomas Hayball. Decoration of the rood screen and its figures, and of the chancel roof, was the work of the Sheffield artist, Henry Taylor Bulmer. The gates to the Blessed Sacrament chapel, the screens that separated the chapel from the chancel, the hearse that covered the

1. Hunter, p. 284; Hadfield, p. 189; *HC* (Sept. 1937), p. 8.
2. de l'Hôpital, p. 531; *The Tablet* (24 Aug. 1872), p. 242.
3. *The Tablet* (25 May 1889), p. 831.

tomb of Fr Pratt, and the exterior gates and railings were executed by James and Charles Ellis of George Street, Sheffield.[1]

Other Furnishings

The following furnishings have been installed subsequent to the opening. The old organ was replaced in 1875 by a fine instrument by Thomas Lewis of London. The case of Austrian oak was designed by J.F. Bentley in collaboration with the architects of the church, and carved by James Erskine Knox. The donor was the Duke of Norfolk. The north side of the organ case was badly damaged by blast from the bomb that destroyed two windows in the Blessed Sacrament chapel in December 1940. Repairs were put in hand at once, but the organ was out of action for three months, during which time a harmonium did service. The new hand-carved panels on the organ case are indistinguishable from the old.[2]

Both of the shrines in the north transept have surfaces of alabaster and Hopton Wood stone, with thirteenth-century columns of Frosterley marble which stood originally in Durham Cathedral, and bear offering tables of Derbyshire fossil marble. The upper portions are carved in wainscot oak, gilded and decorated, with paintings of saints in the panels by Westlake. The figure of the Blessed Virgin Mary, carved in pear wood by Johann Petz of Munich, was acquired in 1850. The base of the shrine was erected in 1868 and the upper part in 1872. The Sacred Heart shrine was completed in 1879. The statue was carved by Boulton of Cheltenham, who executed both shrines from designs of M.E. Hadfield and Son.[3]

The altar of the Norfolk chantry was completed in 1872. The reredos of Caen stone, in the early fourteenth-century style of Beverley and Heckington churches, consists of canopied niches with figures of St Joseph and angels. This was designed by Charles Hadfield and executed by Thomas Earp of Lambeth. The relievo of the death of St Joseph and the other figures were sculptured by Theodore Phyffers. The windows of the Immaculate Conception and the Sacred Heart

1. Hadfield, pp. 65-66, 95, 98, 189.
2. Hadfield, p. 159; de l'Hôpital, p. 623; *HC* (Apr. 1941), p. 4.
3. Hadfield, pp. 89, 144, 163-64; *The Tablet* (1 Feb. 1868), pp. 66-67; *Br* (6 Nov. 1886), p. 662.

were installed by Lavers, Barraud and Westlake.[1]

Individual works not noted above are the reredos of the Mortuary chapel altar, 1850, by Johann Petz, and the Pieta in the north transept, designed by Charles Hadfield from a cast supplied by Pugin and sculptured by Frank Tory in 1887. The lamp in the Blessed Sacrament chapel was given by Charles Hadfield; formerly in the chancel, it was renovated in 1951 by Mr Harry Hurst, long-time bell ringer, in memory of his parents. The paintings of St Winefride in the south transept and St George near the west door are by Westlake.[2]

Subsequent Building Work

At the same time as the Lady chapel was constructed in 1879, the sacristies were extended along Norfolk Row. The sculptured representation of the Annunciation above the door at the corner of Norfolk Street came from the Lambeth workshop of Thomas Earp. The armorial bearings are those of Pope Leo XIII and the Duke of Norfolk. The rectory was built in 1903–1904 from designs of C. and C.M. Hadfield. The statue of the Blessed Virgin is by Alfred Tory.[3]

1. *The Tablet* (24 Aug. 1872), p. 242.
2. Hadfield, pp. 88, 164, 172, 191, 197.
3. *Br* (21 Mar. 1903), p. 314; *The Tablet* (22 Oct. 1904), p. 662.

Chapter 5

SCHOOLS, CEMETERY AND HOSPITAL

St Marie's Schools

The first note found refers to 'a small single room at the back of the priest's house in Norfolk Row' in which was a school for fifty boys and girls.[1] This was very likely founded by Fr George Keasley soon after his arrival in 1830. As seen above in Chapter 3, the house was that built for Fr Rimmer in 1780, which still stands as numbers 4–6 Norfolk Row. Clearly, larger schools were required, and to this end land was leased in Surrey Street at a rent of £14. 4s. per annum from 1833. Here a school is recorded as built in 1835–36 which had 150 boys on the ground floor and 150 girls on the upper floor.[2] These schools were conducted by lay teachers until the advent of the Sisters of Notre Dame in 1855. The Sisters lived initially at Holy Green House on The Moor and taught at St Marie's and St Vincent's schools.

The Surrey Street building was superseded by new schools, for girls in 1858 and for boys in 1878. The new school for girls and infants was built at the corner of St Mary's Road and Sheaf Gardens at a cost of £3,680. The site of half an acre was the gift of the Duke of Norfolk, and His Grace also subscribed to the building fund, which was raised by voluntary contributions, aided by a Privy Council Grant. The foundation stone was laid by the Duchess of Norfolk on 15th September 1857. The construction was of brick with stone facings in the Tudor domestic style that the architect Matthew Hadfield favoured to the end of his life. The present writer attended the infants' department in 1933–35, and can well remember the emphasis there on sound teaching in number, reading, drama, religious knowledge and singing.

1. Arundel, D 85: Schools' Committee's Report to the Duke of Norfolk, 1856.
2. Arundel, D 85; Hadfield, p. 51.

The plan of the building was U-shaped. Two large rooms, 80 by 30 ft, and 52 by 24 ft, were subdivided into classes and joined by a corridor which was entered by a porch fronting St Mary's Road. There were rooms for the teachers and two spacious playgrounds next to the river Sheaf on the southern boundary. The building was badly damaged in the air raid of 12th December 1940, and subsequently demolished. The girls and infants then shared the premises of the boys' school. When the girls moved to their new building in 1858, the boys had the Surrey Street school to themselves. Eventually a new school for boys was opened in Edmund Road on 26th June 1878, at a cost of £6,420. The Duke of Norfolk donated the site and about half the cost of the building, the balance coming from the congregation and the sale of the old school. After a chequered career involving various uses, the Surrey Street building became the Register Office, and was demolished in 1974.[1]

The boys' school, designed by Messrs Hadfield and Son, was in the neo-Tudor style, realized in brick and stone and roofed with Broseley tiles. Two large schoolrooms (70 by 25 ft, later subdivided) and two classrooms (26 by 20 ft) provided accommodation for 400 boys. A spacious octagonal stone staircase occupied one corner, giving access to both storeys, to the staff rooms, to the caretaker's quarters, and to the playground. It was carried up as a tower and surmounted by a lead spire in which the school bell hung. Next to this was the principal entrance, an arched doorway with the arms of Pope Leo XIII and the Duke of Norfolk, flanking a statue supplied by Messrs Boulton of Cheltenham of the Blessed Virgin Mary with the Infant Saviour. On the Leadmill Road corner of the site was a house for the schoolmaster, which was later occupied by the De La Salle Brothers, who taught here and at St Vincent's School.[2]

Owing to the destruction of the Sheaf Gardens premises, the two schools were accommodated from January 1941 in the Edmund Road building, the boys upstairs and the girls downstairs. Eventually the schools were amalgamated. Following the implementation of the 1944 Education Act, children over the age of eleven went to the various

1. Account Book of Canon Fisher; Hadfield, pp. 132-33; for the school plan see Arundel, S 484/6/3; *Br* (26 Sept. 1857), pp. 553-54; an enlargement to the school is recorded in *The Tablet* (2 Nov. 1872), p. 564.

2. Hadfield, p. 162; *SRI* (26 June 1878), p. 3; *The Tablet* (29 June 1878), p. 820; *Br* (20 July 1878), p. 762.

secondary schools, and St Marie's became a primary school. A new building was planned in Granville Road, but owing to the requirements of city-wide provision, the new school was finally sited at Oakbrook in Fulwood Road. The architects Messrs Weightman and Bullen altered their first plan, producing a flexible design adapted to the sloping site. Uppermost is the main entrance on a level with Fulwood Road; below this is the junior department and lower still the infants'. The central focus is a forum for use by infants and juniors; and beyond is a sports hall with changing facilities. Adjacent to the hall is the school kitchen. The teaching areas are grouped around open, practical work spaces, and on a terraced site facing south are playing fields and games areas. The new building was opened in September 1972. After a year of social usage, the Edmund Road school was damaged by fire, and had to be pulled down.[1]

The Sisters of Notre Dame

It was Canon Scully, with the help of Mr Robert Gainsford, Matthew Hadfield and others, who arranged for the Sisters of Notre Dame to come to Sheffield. Holy Green House on The Moor, the capacious former residence of T.B. Holy, was taken for them. The Sisters arrived in Sheffield from Liverpool on 25th July 1855, and in a short time opened a school for young ladies in the convent and taught in the girls' schools of St Marie's and St Vincent's.

In 1861 the Sisters purchased two semi-detached houses in Cavendish Street, which were enlarged and adapted to the uses of a school. Some houses in Victoria Street were also acquired as a residence for pupil teachers, and the school moved there from Holy Green House on 28th April 1862. The Sisters also took charge of St William's School in Lee Croft on 19th January 1863. Later, there were extensions to the convent school, including a chapel. A French priest, Fr Charles Leteux, who was at St Marie's from 1888 until 1896, served as school chaplain.[2]

1. *Cathedral*, pp. 24-25, 31, 34-35; *CBR.N* (1968), p. 332; *CBR.N* (1970), p. 282. The architects in 1972 were Mr and Mrs Brown for Messrs Weightman and Bullen of York; the contractors Messrs Bailey and Martyn of Sheffield.

2. *Foundations of the Sisters of Notre Dame* (Liverpool: Philip, Son and Nephew, 1895), pp. 93-95; Hadfield, pp. 119-20; *The Tablet* (31 May 1862), p. 342; *CD* (1859, 1887-97).

Plate 10 Oakbrook Chapel, exterior, 1956

In 1919 the sisters and boarders moved to Oakbrook on Fulwood
Road. A large Italianate house standing in extensive grounds,
Oakbrook had been built about 1860 by the architects Flockton and
Son for the industrialist Mark Firth. Extensions to the house, includ-
ing the addition of a *porte-cochère*, were made prior to the visit of the
Prince and Princess of Wales in 1875. A school was built in the
grounds in 1935, which became an annexe to that at Cavendish Street.[1]
Oakbrook's domestic chapel (in the former ballroom) was superseded
by a new chapel opened by Bishop Heenan on 8th December 1956.
The architect J.H. Langtry-Langton employed a neo-Romanesque style
in keeping with the Italianate of the house, realized in coursed and
snecked wall stones and ashlar blocks, and roofed with Westmorland
slates. The chapel's interior has a nave and aisles of five bays, with

1. *Sheffield Illustrated*, vol. 2 (1885), pp. 10-11. The architect of the school of
1935 was Henry C. Smart of London; the contractor was Arthur F. White of
Chesterfield. See *Sheffield Telegraph* (23 Nov. 1935), p. 11.

chancel, sacristy and west gallery. The chapel is connected to the house by a cell block, with separate quarters for the chaplain.[1]

Plate 11 Oakbrook Chapel, interior, 1956

With the decision to convert the High School from direct grant to voluntary-aided status as a mixed comprehensive school with a sixth form, extensions to the building were required. A beginning was made by J.H. Langtry-Langton in 1977–78, with a link building between the school and the house in Riverdale Road. However, it was always desired that Notre Dame School should be on only one site, at Oakbrook, and this became possible in 1987. At that time the Notre Dame convent at Parbold was adapted to take the elderly sisters, who moved there from Sheffield. The Order then placed the house at Oakbrook, with most of the land, on the market to the diocese, which bought it with the help of a DES grant. Buildings including a sports hall were added to the existing school, enabling all the students at Cavendish Street to move to Oakbrook. The architects for this work were Messrs Rochford and Partners. Eventually the Fulwood Road buildings (including the former convent) housed the whole school, and

1. *CBR.N* (1954), pp. 203-204; (1956), pp. 259, 261.

Cavendish Street was closed and demolished in 1988. The Sisters of Notre Dame continued to conduct the school, and moved to a new home at 31 Ashdell Road in May 1988.[1] Owing to the shortage of vocations, however, the Sisters left Sheffield in 1991, having served education in the city for 136 years.

All Saints School

In addition to Notre Dame High School and De La Salle College, other secondary modern schools were founded in the city. In due course, parish schools became primary schools, and at the age of eleven children left these for Notre Dame, De La Salle, St Peter's, Parsons Cross (1959), St Paul's (Granville Road, 1962) or St John Fisher (Handsworth, 1965).[2]

The site in Granville Road originally designated for St Marie's Primary School was utilized instead for a new secondary modern school. Known as The Farm Grounds, the site has a history connected with the Sheffield Catholic mission. When the 11th Duke of Norfolk had The Lord's House pulled down in 1814, the agent moved his home and office to The Farm, where some rebuilding took place in 1824. Following the accession of Henry Granville as 14th Duke in 1856, The Farm was converted to an occasional residence. There was a new dining room and a domestic chapel over the gateway. An office wing was built, terminated by a square tower with an oriel turret. These extensions were the work of Weightman, Hadfield and Goldie. At the same time (1857), Beech Hill was built in Norfolk Park Road nearby as a new residence for the agent.

When the Midland Railway arrived in 1870, a single line was sunk beneath the ducal grounds. However, the peaceful rural character of the estate was already being compromized by the proximity of busy roads, and so Duke Henry took Beech Hill as his occasional residence. From 1898 the LMS Railway leased The Farm for use as offices. The house was finally pulled down when Mgr Dinn acquired the land for a school in 1959.[3]

1. *CBR.N* (1966), p. 330; (1977), p. 118; (1978), p. 65.
2. *Cathedral*, pp. 30, 36.
3. Hadfield, p. 177; Hunter, p. 230; *Cathedral*, p. 30; Welsh; *The Tablet* (27 Aug. 1859), p. 559.

Plate 12 The Farm, 1859

St Paul's School was begun in March 1961 and opened in September 1962, with an intake of 600 pupils on a well-wooded site arranged for winter and summer sports. It was designed in three compact blocks of two and four storeys of classrooms, practical rooms and laboratories. It was also graced by two statues, moulded in fibreglass by C. and M. Blakeman, of Christ on the Cross and the conversion of St Paul. The architects were Messrs Hadfield, Cawkwell and Davidson; the main contractors J.F. Finnegan and Company; and the overall cost was £256,623. Changes in educational organization soon resulted in the amalgamation of De La Salle with St Paul's, which changed its name to All Saints School. By 1980 De La Salle was phased out altogether and St Paul's had extra accommodation. This included a sixth form block, a new art department, a TV studio, and the alteration of existing buildings. The architects for this work were John Rochford and Partners, the main contractor C.R. Pursehouse Ltd, and the cost was £115,000.[1]

In 1991 the De La Salle library was added to the main building and formally opened by Bishop Moverley on 8th June. The architect of this extension was Mr Anthony Tranmer of John Rochford and Partners; the contractors were DVR Building Services of Dronfield.

St Marie's Hall

A Catholic Association was founded in Sheffield in 1872 to provide recreation in the evenings for young men. The premises at 20 Paradise Square contained a library and news, billiard and coffee rooms, together with a spacious room in which lectures and concerts were occasionally given. Canon Walshaw blessed the premises on 21st January 1873, and the inaugural meeting was addressed by Archbishop Manning and the Duke of Norfolk. For want of viable numbers, however, the association did not flourish, and it was wound up after about five years. Hadfield asserted that it was started before its time, and hoped that it would be revived.

The men's club was revived when Dean Dolan acquired the premises of the Temperance Hall in Townhead Street. This had been built in 1814 and extended with a spacious porch and three entrances in 1878. Two large rooms now served as a parish hall and the men's

1. *Architect and Building News* (17 July 1963), p. 100; *CBR.N* (1963), p. 332; (1964), p. 416; (1977), p. 104; (1980), p. 133.

club. Here such functions as school and parish plays and concerts, dances, bazaars and meetings took place. However, during the Second World War, the premises were rented to the factory next door as a canteen, and they never reverted to regular parochial use. St Marie's Hall was demolished in 1979. Under the administration of Mgr Sullivan, the Old Rectory in Norfolk Row was demolished, only the Georgian front being retained. The rebuilding, assisted by a generous legacy of Mrs Beatrice Houlden, resulted in the facility of a splendidly decorated and comfortable new parish hall on the upper floor, with offices and business premises occupying the remainder of the building.[1]

The Little Sisters of the Poor

In 1882 the St Marie's Conference of the Society of St Vincent de Paul, in co-operation with Canon Walshaw, arranged for the Little Sisters of the Poor to open a home for the aged in Sheffield. Their first home was a small villa residence at 80 Duchess Road. Clearly, larger premises were needed, and through the munificence of the Duke of Norfolk, a site close by was obtained, lying between Farm Road and Queens Road. The foundation stone of St Elizabeth's Home was laid by Duke Henry on 3rd June 1889. On 17th March 1890 the home was formally opened and blessed by Dr Gordon, coadjutor Bishop of Leeds in the presence of the Duke, Canon Walshaw and Dr Cauwenberghe. It was designed to accommodate 150 aged persons. However, only the first part was built, a block 120 ft by 40 ft two storeys high, in the Italian style; this had accommodation for about 75 aged men and women. The architect was Francis William Tasker of London, who was regularly employed by the Order to design their Homes. The builders were Messrs Grantham and Whelan. In 1908 the home moved to new premises in Heeley Bank Road, designed by Edmund Winder. It flourished there until it was closed in 1980.[2]

1. Hadfield, pp. 149, 161; *Cathedral*, pp. 17, 37.
2. Hadfield, pp. 148-49; *SRI* (4 June 1889), p. 6; (18 Mar. 1890), p. 2.

Intake Cemetery Chapel

The City Road (formerly Intake) Cemetery was opened in 1881. The site of 50 acres was purchased by the town from the Duke of Norfolk for £13,625. Work on the layout of the ground, the two Protestant churches, the offices and the sextons' houses had commenced in 1873 to designs by Hadfield and Son. The ground was allocated in due proportion for the use of the Church of England, Nonconformists and Roman Catholics.

The portion allocated to the Catholics was consecrated by Bishop Cornthwaite on 9th June 1881. It has an entrance and lodge in Manor Lane, a mere stone's throw from the remains of Sheffield Manor with its associations with Cardinal Wolsey and Mary Queen of Scots. The chapel dedicated to St Michael was provided by the Duke of Norfolk and blessed by Dean Dolan on 11th October 1900. Some 60 feet in length and built of Worrall stone, the chapel was designed in a simple early Gothic style, in a centralized plan which derives from the Holy Sepulchre at Jerusalem. Thus the altar is placed in the centre of a hexagonal colonnade which supports a lantern, and the aisle is continued around the altar. The architects were Messrs C. and C.M. Hadfield, and the builders were Messrs D. O'Neill and Son.[1]

Claremont Hospital

A Catholic Nursing Home standing in spacious private grounds in Claremont Place was opened by Bishop Cowgill in 1921. Supporting his Lordship were Bishop Keatinge, Fr Bede Jarrett, OP, Canon Dolan and Fr A. Collingwood, SJ. The Home was the first of its kind to be opened in the district, and since its inception has been under the care of the Sisters of Mercy. Now designated Claremont Hospital, it was moved to its present site in Sandygate Road in 1953. From the beginning the chapel has been served from the churches of St Marie and St Francis.[2]

1. *SRI* (28 Mar. 1881), p. 3; (10 June 1881), p. 2; (12 Oct. 1900), p. 7; *The Tablet* (20 Oct. 1900), p. 632.
2. *The Tablet* (9 July 1921), p. 60.

Chapter 6

EARLY FOUNDATIONS:
ST BEDE; ST VINCENT; ST ANN

St Bede's, Rotherham

Rotherham was the first missionary offshoot of the Sheffield chapel. Traditionally, Fr Christopher Gradwell, who was chaplain at Sheffield from 1736 to 1758, initiated a monthly Mass there. In 1841 the Catholics of Rotherham petitioned Bishop Briggs, asking for help to build a church. They said that they were about a hundred in number, and since about 1838 they had leased the Old Theatre in the town and used it as a Catholic chapel, where Mass was said by priests from Sheffield. The lease of the theatre was running out, and a Protestant gentleman of the town, Mr Benjamin Badger, had offered them the gift of a piece of freehold land on which to build a chapel. They were trying to raise money among themselves to meet the expenses of building, but 'as one of the poorest of the poor congregations of Catholics in this country' they asked the Bishop's help. The priest who signed the petition, together with 69 members of the congregation, was Fr Marcus Supple, assistant at Sheffield.

The foundation stone was laid by Bishop Briggs on 29th July 1841, and St Bede's Church was opened on 5th October 1842. This was the first church by Weightman and Hadfield to be designed in strict mediaeval form, having nave, chancel, porch and sacristy in the Decorated style, and as such was singled out for praise by Pugin in his *Present State*. The cost was £1,200, defrayed by subscription. A presbytery was built on the north side soon after the church was opened. An aisle and baptistery were added in 1920–21 to designs of C.M. Hadfield.[1]

1. *Catholic Monthly* (July 1950); Kelly, p. 335; Hadfield, p. 61; *Catholic Annual Register* (1850), p. 108; A.W.N. Pugin, *Present State of Ecclesiastical Architecture in England* (London: Dolman, 1842), pp. 107-108.

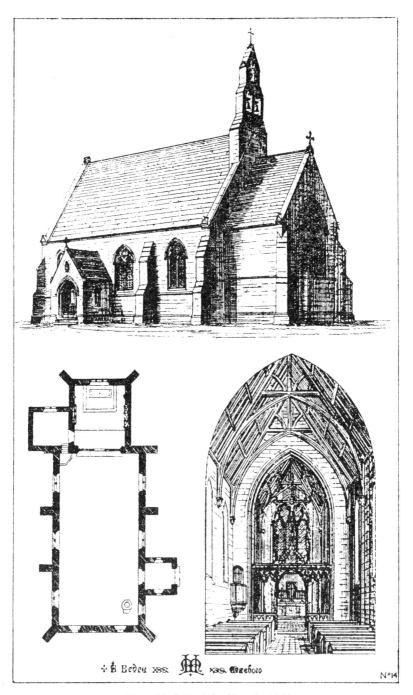

Plate 13 St Bede's Church, 1842

St Vincent's Mission

By the time that St Marie's was built, a large number of Irish people were settled in Sheffield. Driven from their homeland by famine and attracted here by the prospect of employment, most of them lived in the Crofts district. Arrangements had to be made for their spiritual welfare and this Fr Scully did, with the provision of a school chapel and the introduction to Sheffield of the Congregation of the Mission of St Vincent de Paul.

At this point it is necessary to relate the facts concerning a curious diversion which occurred in the late 1840s, for during the building of St Marie's an unauthorized project arose to erect a church in Queen Street. A committee of men leased land from the Town Trustees and employed the local firm of architects, Messrs Flockton, Son and Lee, to design a church. They did this because they feared in good faith that St Marie's would not be able to accommodate the Catholic population of the town. They genuinely sought, moreover, to prevent the luring away of Catholics from their faith.

There was some substance to their misgivings. In Catholic churches throughout the land, congregational space was allocated on a basis of charges made through bench rents or at the door. The system inevitably generated graded accommodation for various types of worshipper—the wealthy, the middle-class and the poor. In chapels of moderate size, the poor would be relegated to the back, near the entrance, without benches. This was the case in the New Chapel in Norfolk Row, as attested by the plan for the western extension made in 1838 (Sheffield City Library AP55). The misgivings of certain parishioners were therefore understandable. Yet it must be remembered that they had neither episcopal nor sacerdotal permission for the projected church. Fr William Parsons, rector of the Sheffield mission, appeared unable to control the situation. He was suspended by Bishop Briggs, and after an investigation, was reinstated elsewhere in the Northern District. In the meantime building work on the illicit church was abandoned for want of sufficient funds. Fr Parsons was replaced at Sheffield by Fr Edmund Scully, who defused the situation by presiding over the opening of St Marie's church and founding the mission of St Vincent's.[1]

---

1. *Catholic Monthly* (Aug. 1950); Ushaw College, Robert Tate correspondence

St Vincent's School Chapel

At Fr Scully's behest, Matthew Hadfield sought land on which to develop a mission in the Crofts. He discovered an eligible plot at the top of White Croft which he purchased for £1,000 with the assistance of a Protestant friend. Here a school chapel was erected at a cost of about £1,800, and opened on 22nd August 1853.

Meanwhile, Fr Scully had been negotiating with the Vincentian Fathers at Phibsborough with a view to their taking charge of the new mission. He took 90 Garden Street as a Community House for them, and on 13th November three priests and one lay brother arrived in Sheffield. Before taking up residence they stayed with Fr Scully for a time. On the first Sunday of Advent Fr Michael Burke, the Superior, said the first Mass in the school chapel.[1]

Fr Burke decided to press on quickly with the erection of a permanent church. With the help of substantial contributions and regular weekly collections, it was possible to begin building by the spring of 1856. The foundation stone of St Vincent's Church was laid by the Vicar General, Fr Joseph Render, on 25th March. It was not intended to build the south aisle at once, but with funds coming in rapidly, work on the aisle went ahead. Thus the church which was opened on 16th December 1856 consisted of nave, chancel and south aisle, and cost £3,300.[2]

The original design for St Vincent's Church came from the firm styled Weightman, Hadfield and Goldie. Whilst still a scholar at St Cuthbert's College, Ushaw, George Goldie (1828–1887) had sought a pupillage with the leading architect Pugin. Pugin recommended him to Weightman and Hadfield, with whom he was articled for five years. Then Goldie joined the partnership, and from 1856 to 1858 he was in charge of the firm's ecclesiastical work. Thus George Goldie was the actual architect of St Vincent's Church.[3]

The prevailing interest in French mediaeval architecture had a decided and permanent effect on Goldie's work. There was little scope for expensive details in Fr Burke's modest commission, but at

(20 Apr. 1850).
1.   Hadfield, p. 116; *Catholic Monthly* (Sept. 1950).
2.   Hadfield, pp. 126-27.
3.   Welsh.

St Vincent's, Goldie abandoned the type of straight-ended chancel previously favoured by Pugin, and designed a shallow, continental-style apse.[1]

Plate 14 St Vincent's Church, 1856

Over the years, several structural additions have been made to St Vincent's Church. The Sacred Heart chapel off the south aisle was built in 1890 by Mrs Mary Ann Foster; the north aisle was built in 1899, together with the carriage approach from Solly Street, at a cost of £3,000; the architects were C. and C.M. Hadfield, and the builder D. O'Neill and Son. (The blank arcade over the built-in confessionals

1.   This was the first of many churches with French details by Goldie, e.g. St Peter, Scarborough (1958); St Peter, Ipswich (1860); St Wilfrid, York (1863); Our Lady of Victories, Kensington (1869); and The Faithful Virgin, Norwood (1871).

echoes a similar arcade in front of the Sacred Heart chapel opposite.) The lower stage of the tower containing an entrance on its south side was built to a height of 40 ft in 1870; it was completed in 1911 to a new design by Charles Hadfield. Following damage by enemy action in 1940, the sacristy was rebuilt in 1959, and the south-east chapel of the Holy Souls added in 1964 to designs of Hadfield, Cawkwell and Davidson. The west gallery with its organ by T.C. Wilcock was added in 1953.[1]

St Vincent's Presbytery

The Presbytery in Garden Street served until about 1867, when the priests moved to 142 Broad Lane. The old presbytery served as St Vincent's Grammar School in 1878–79, and thereafter as the convent of the Sisters of Charity. The new presbytery was situated at the corner of Broad Lane and Red Hill and was named St Vincent's House.

By July 1878, the purpose-built clergy house at the corner of Solly Street and Garden Street was ready for occupation. This was provided by the Duke of Norfolk at a cost of £11,000.[2] An imposing building, six bays wide and four storeys tall, it was designed by Hadfield and Son. Realized in brick, its Renaissance style was reminiscent of the Order's seventeenth-century traditions. In a niche was a statue of St Vincent and the legend 'Evangelizare pauperibus misit me'. The ample accommodation included two parlours, refectory and porter's room on the ground floor, chapel with vestry, library and community room on the first floor, and two storeys above containing fourteen clergy rooms. The clergy moved to St Joseph's, Walkley, and the presbytery was sold in 1988.[3]

1. Hadfield, p. 147; *St Vincent's*; *Br* (11 June 1898), p. 571; (9 Sept. 1899), p. 246; (13 Sept. 1912), pp. 313, 315; *BN* (15 Sept. 1899), p. 10; *SRI* (2 Sept. 1899), p. 10; (11 Sept. 1899), p. 7; *SDT* (30 Oct. 1911), p. 9; *CBR.N* (1959), pp. 150-51; (1964), pp. 146-47.

2. The builders' specifications included best ashlar exterior of Turner's quarry stone at Worrall, porch of best Hollington stone, staircase of Hopton Wood stone from Wirksworth, Peake's Staffordshire tiles, Robinson's or other approved bricks. See Sheffield City Library LD 2353.

3. Hadfield, pp. 162-63; *St Vincent's*; *SRI* (6 July 1878), p. 2; Welsh.

St Vincent's Schools

Through the good offices of Fr Burke, the Sisters of Charity came to work in St Vincent's mission in 1857. Their first home was 157 Solly Street; later they were at 222 Solly Street at the corner of Corn Hill; and in 1878 they moved to St Vincent's House, the former clergy house in Broad Lane.

The girls' school had flourished since 1853; the boys' school since 1854. From 1855 to 1863 the sisters of Notre Dame taught the girls; then the Sisters of Charity. In 1858, Fr Burke placed the infants' department in a separate building to the north of the church, adapted from a block of houses. Since this was quite inadequate for 300 infants, Fr Burke was urged by Her Majesty's Inspectors to build a new boys' school, and to give their portion of the original school to the girls and infants. The foundation stone of the new boys' school was laid by Fr Hickey on 21st October 1863.

In Fr Brady's time (1892–1897) a new infants' department was built alongside the boys' school, the former building soon giving way to the site of the church's new north aisle. Following the destruction of their school by bombing in December 1940, the girls moved into part of the infants' building. Eventually the girls' and infants' schools were amalgamated. Extra accommodation was added in 1949 following the raising of the school-leaving age and the influx of senior children from St Marie's.

The two schools, for girls and infants, and boys, were amalgamated in 1963 into a junior mixed and infants' school. From that time, children over eleven went to one of the secondary or grammar schools—Notre Dame, De La Salle, St Peter's or St Paul's. Owing to falling numbers, St Vincent's School was closed in 1989.[1]

St Joseph's, Walkley

In 1861 a meeting was held at York with the setting up of a reformatory for Catholic girls in view. The sole existing establishment of this kind, at Arnos Court near Bristol, was fully occupied, and Sheffield

---

1. Hadfield, pp. 128-29; *Catholic Education Council Handbook* (1960-1988); *St Vincent's.*

was selected as a central location in the north for a similar institution. The Sisters of Charity offered to undertake its management, if they

Plate 15 St Vincent's Church and School, 1856

were provided with a suitable building. The committee of the Yorkshire Catholic Reformatory School approved the purchase of a property at Howard Hill, Sheffield. It consisted of two acres of land and a stone-built house occupied by Mr Wright's Boarding School. The property was purchased for £1,450 and was blessed as St Joseph's Home on 15th August 1861. A new stone-built wing, designed by Hadfield and Son and constructed by W. Reynolds at a cost of £1,700, was opened on 26th October 1864. This consisted of refectory, schoolroom and workroom; and above, a dormitory, infirmary and sick room. Five Sisters of Charity lived in the old house. The home

Plate 16 Church of St Joseph, Walkley, 1871

could now accommodate 100 girls, and served the six northern dioceses of Beverley, Liverpool, Salford, Nottingham, Shrewsbury and Hexham.

The chapel was commenced in May 1871 and, owing to the illness of Bishop Cornthwaite, was dedicated by Canon Walshaw on 21st April 1872. M.E. Hadfield and Son were the architects and John Pearson was Clerk of Works. The slope of the ground facilitated the construction of a schoolroom beneath the chapel. The stone-built chapel is designed in the Early English phase of the Gothic style. It consists of an unaisled nave of four bays, with bell turret, west gallery, apsidal chancel and roof of six arched principals on corbels. For the sisters and the girls there were entrances from the (ritual) west and south, and an access passage for the public on the north. The original stained glass by Lavers, Barraud and Westlake has now disappeared, all the windows bearing multicoloured small panes. In the elaborate stone reredos is a plaque to Robert John Gainsford (†1870), the virtual founder of the establishment.

Eventually the reformatory became a hospital for the mentally ill. This was closed in 1983. The hospital was then demolished, the chapel retained for public use, the convent converted to a presbytery for the priests of St Vincent's, and much of the surrounding land sold for building. Across the road, St Joseph's School in Howard Hill was opened in 1889 and closed in 1981.[1]

Rivelin Cemetery

Following the closure of the burial ground in Norfolk Row in 1847, there was no specifically Catholic cemetery in Sheffield. The General Cemetery had been open since 1836 and Catholics could be buried there. But for those desiring interment in consecrated ground, the nearest place was at St. Bede's Church, Rotherham. Here, for instance, the Sheffield Catholic artist Henry Taylor Bulmer was interred in 1857.

Eventually an initiative of several Irishmen enabled Fr Burke and Fr Barlow to provide a Catholic cemetery. Four acres of land charmingly situated on the hillside that overlooks Rivelin valley were bought from the Wilson family for £600 and enclosed at a cost of £250. Following Government sanction of the site and its approval as a burial ground by the Home Secretary, the cemetery was opened on St Michael's Day, 29th September 1862. A temporary chapel was erected, and blessed by Fr Burke on 26th October 1863. Since that time, Mass has been said monthly for the repose of the souls of the faithful departed.

On 9th May 1878, the present St Michael's chapel was opened by

1. Hadfield, p. 137; *St Vincent's*; *SRI* (19 Jan. 1861), p. 6; (27 Oct. 1864), p. 3; (22 Apr. 1872), p. 4; *BN* (3 May 1872), p. 363.

Bishop Cornthwaite. The cost was £2,000, and Mr and Mrs Foster were the patrons. M.E. Hadfield and Son (whose family grave lies to the east of the chapel) were the architects, and the builder was M.J. Dowling. St Michael's is a charming composition in the Early English phase of Gothic, built of hammer-dressed Greenmoor wall stone, with Worrall stone dressings, and roofed with Staffordshire tiles. In plan it consists of an unaisled nave with apsidal east end, 22 ft wide and 72 ft long internally, with a south porch and north-east sacristy. In the gable of the porch a niche contains a figure of St Michael slaying the dragon. In the western bell-turret, which is 60 ft high, hangs a bell weighing 5 cwt cast in 1877 by Mears and Stainbank. The altar is of polished marble and veined alabaster, with a figure beneath of the dead Christ in white alabaster, sculpted by Boulton of Cheltenham. The chancel floor is laid with patterned encaustic tiles, the choir seats are of oak, and the Stations of the Cross of terra cotta, in high relief. The three east windows of the Risen Christ, the Blessed Virgin, and St John were designed by John Francis Bentley and executed by Lavers, Barraud and Westlake.

In 1884, through the further patronage of Mr and Mrs Foster, and at a cost of £430, the chapel was further enriched to designs of Charles Hadfield and Nathaniel Westlake with the installation of the west window (in memory of Fr James Fitzgerald †1883), the Sienese crucifix and the wall paintings of the four Resurrections.[1]

Other Vincentian Foundations

Owing to the shortage of priests, the mission at Stannington was closed by Bishop Smith, and following the death of Fr Rimmer the weekly Monday Masses were discontinued from 1828. With the advent of the Vincentian priests, Fr Burke renewed in 1854 the celebration of Mass at Revell Grange. In 1858 the chapel, rebuilt and enlarged by Mr Sutton, was reopened as a missionary station. Here Mass was said on Sundays and holy days until, owing to a change of ownership, the chapel was closed in 1929.[2]

1.   Hadfield, pp. 138-39; de l'Hôpital, p. 531; *St Vincent's*; *Br* (25 May 1878), p. 549; *SRI* (11 May 1878), p. 3; *British Architect* (12 Aug. 1892), p. 112.
2.   Hadfield, pp. 18-20; *St Vincent's*.

West End

S· Michael's
Cemetery
Chapel

Rivelin Glen
M · E · Hadfield & Son
Architects

The Altar

Plate 17 St Michael's Chapel, Rivelin, 1878

The parish of Deepcar is descended from the mission of Bolsterstone. From the Jesuit house at Spinkhill, Fr Ignatius Brooke served the Sheffield mission from 1711 to about 1735. His patrons in Sheffield were the agents to the Duke of Norfolk—first John Shireburn, and from 1726 Benjamin Blackburn. Fr Brooke also developed a mission at Bolsterstone, since Mr Blackburn had a house there. He was probably succeeded by Fr James Foxe, SJ (alias Pole or Poole) until 1739. Foley's *Records* inform us that

> Three small donations were made in or about 1739 by Mrs Margaret Blackburne, Mrs Mary Blackburne, and Mrs Anne Hague, the interest to be given to any member of the Society serving in that neighbourhood . . . A sum of £50 is also named in an ancient paper, the interest to be applied 'for a refreshment for the communicants'—a great charity in those days, when the poor had sometimes ten or twenty miles to walk to their duties and the priest was too poor to help them.[1]

The last priest thought to be associated with Bolsterstone is Fr John Boarman, SJ, following his ordination in 1759. But Hadfield asserts that the Bolsterstone mission was kept up until early in the nineteenth century, at Spinkhouse, the residence of the Smith family; and that St Ann's at Deepcar may be said to have replaced Bolsterstone.

As early as 1853, the presence of about 200 Catholics engaged in the terra cotta works and collieries around Deepcar came to Fr Burke's notice. Without a chapel, only occasional visits to catechize in the larger cottages were then possible. However, a site was found for a chapel and house, and the foundation stone was laid on 15th August 1859. The building, of stone in the early Gothic style, was completed in May 1860 to designs of Hadfield and Goldie.[2]

The Catholic Young Men's Society has flourished since it was founded by Fr Burke in 1854. This was the first beginning of the society in England. The former works of Messrs Spencer were purchased and adapted in 1896. These premises, opened by the Duke of Norfolk, included a large billiard room, smoking room, reading room and library. The air raid of December 1940 demolished the club, which then had quarters in Garden Street and Solly Street. Since the closure of the Youth Centre, the club has occupied the centre's former

1. Vol. V, p. 708.
2. Hadfield, pp. 20, 21; *St Vincent's*; Kelly, p. 152; *CRS* 13, p. 178; *CRS* 70, pp. 36, 43, 96; *BN* (2 June 1860), p. 253.

premises in the Old Croft Board School building in Solly Street.

St Vincent's Hall in Solly Street was erected in 1910. Councillor and Mrs P.J. Benson were generous patrons. Two houses, one of them the former convent of the Sisters of Charity, were adapted to form part of the street frontage. Following damage to the church in the blitz, the hall served as a temporary church from December 1940 to Easter Day 1942. Various parochial activities have endowed these premises with happy memories for very many people, not least among them being the presence of St Vincent's Youth Centre, and the numerous productions of the Columba Operatic Society and other groups.[1]

The University Chaplaincy has existed since 1952. The first chaplain, Dr Gerard Shannon, CM, resided at St Vincent's presbytery for a few months while he sought premises nearer the university. Eventually 7 Wellesley Road was bought and renamed Padley House. The modest structural alterations required for adaptation to the uses of a chapel were undertaken by Messrs D. O'Neill and Son.

Our Lady of the Miraculous Medal. The Crookes district of St Vincent's parish has the chapel of ease of Our Lady of the Miraculous Medal. A redundant Methodist chapel, erected in 1836 in School Road, was acquired and opened for Catholic use in 1957. There were extensions by the architect John Rochford in 1977. The chapel consists of a rectangular room with porch and adjacent rooms used as priests' and boys' sacristies. The long walls contain four bays of round-headed windows. No structural distinction for a chancel is apparent at the (ritual) east end; the altar is at the time of writing placed in the centre of the long north wall. A range of ancillary rooms in two storeys stands to the east. The chapel is served by the priests of St Vincent's parish.[2]

1.   Hadfield, p. 119; *St Vincent's* ; *The Tablet* (14 Nov. 1896), p. 796.
2.   *CBR.N* (1977), p. 209.

Plate 18 Church of Our Lady, School Road, 1957

Chapter 7

FOUNDATIONS WEST:
ST WILLIAM; THE SACRED HEART

St William's Church

Close as St Marie's and St Vincent's churches were to one another, Canon Fisher felt it necessary to make further spiritual provision for those who dwelt in the Crofts. Thus, practically mid-way between the two churches, he founded in 1863 the chapel and schools of St William.

Matthew Hadfield was fortunate in obtaining an old Independent chapel which was now redundant. This stood near the top of Lee Croft, on the west side. Through a Protestant friend, Mr Hadfield purchased the premises for £1,000. With the chapel came complete schools for boys and girls, a master's house and lecture rooms, all of which could not have been built for less than £3,000. Mr Hadfield remodelled the chapel's interior, forming a spacious sanctuary with a richly gilt reredos and tabernacle. The altar was formerly used in the New Chapel in Norfolk Row, and had seen service at the commencement of St Vincent's mission.

St William's chapel of ease was blessed and opened by Bishop Cornthwaite on 11th January 1863. On the 19th, the Sisters of Notre Dame took charge of St William's schools. New schools for about 800 girls and infants were added to the site in 1870 by M.E. Hadfield and Son, at a cost of £800. St William's was served by priests from St Marie's, except for a short period when it had its own chaplains: Fr Patrick Kennedy in 1865–66, and Fr Martin Kelly in 1866–70; latterly he lived at 5 Paradise Square.[1]

In 1905 St William's moved to its present site in Ecclesall Road.

1. Hadfield, pp. 137-38; *The Tablet* (4 Oct. 1862), p. 630; (24 Jan. 1863), p. 54; *BN* (2 Dec. 1870), p. 419; Paine's Plan of Sheffield, 1822.

The old property was acquired by the Sheffield Corporation in connection with clearance of the older parts of the Crofts. Money received for the site was applied to the new church. The foundation stone had been laid on 26th November 1904, and the small mission church was opened on 8th June 1905. The architects were Charles Hadfield and his son Charles Matthew Hadfield. Then in 1925 the nave and chancel were transformed into chancel and vestry, and a nave and aisle were added at right angles to them, increasing the seating accommodation from 100 to 400. The cost was £3,000; the architects were Hadfield and Cawkwell, and the builders were D. O'Neill and Son. Both the original church and its extension were opened by Bishop Cowgill.

Plate 19 St William's Church, 1925

In 1931, Canon Dolan and the congregation together agreed on converting the mission to an independent parish. Fr Thomas Molony became first parish priest in 1932. The presbytery and parish hall were built at this time. The major undertaking of a new roof in 1970–71 supplied the appearance of a practically new church. The old roof had required constant attention; moreover, a row of piers impeded the view of the chancel from the aisle. The architects John Rochford and Partners designed a new, copper-covered roof, supported by columns outside the existing walls. The result is a *tour de force* of well-lit space, uncluttered by internal piers. Since it was not possible to obtain sufficient natural light at wall level, the two halves of the roof were contrived to meet via a long clerestory, furnishing an unimpeded view of the chancel and chapel.[1] At the same time, the interior wall surfaces were plastered and painted white, the ceiling was finished with boarding, the floor relaid, and the heating and benching renewed. The work was completed in October 1971, at an approximate cost of £30,000.

The following year were installed the altar, tabernacle table, and font, in Swedish green marble; the sanctuary floor finished in white marble; stained glass memorial windows reset in a new vestibule; a sculpted crucifix prepared for the sanctuary wall; and the existing statue of St William mounted on a corbel adjacent to the entrance. Subsequent furnishings include the Stations of the Cross, of panels of glass fired on to stone, signed Caudril; and the chancel south window, 'The Tree of Life', signed Paul Quail, 1987.[2]

Mylnhurst Convent School

The Sisters of Mercy took over Mylnhurst, the former home of the Walsh family in Button Hill, and opened an independent school there in 1937. The original house, much of which is now converted to classrooms, had been erected in 1883, in a domestic Gothic style with an embattled tower.

The chief addition to the school has been the chapel, completed in June 1962 to the designs of John Rochford and opened by Bishop Dwyer. Its external walls are of stone, harmonizing happily with the old building. A new sacristy connects the chapel to the convent and adjacent living quarters for a chaplain or visiting priest. The chapel can accommodate the sisters and the schoolchildren—at present 170 boys and girls aged 3 to 11. It consists of a nave of four bays, chancel and west gallery, panelled in oak; the altar and communion rails are in Travertine and Vert St Denis marbles; the grisaille windows were

1. *SDT* (28 Nov. 1904), p. 8; (21 Oct. 1925), p. 3; *SRI* (9 June 1905), p. 8; *Br* (11 Feb. 1927), pp. 243, 247.
2. *CBR.N* (1970), pp. 300-301, 303; (1971), p. 362; (1972), pp. 144-45, 147.

designed by Patrick Reyntiens; the Stations of the Cross are Austrian work; and the Crucifix and Madonna and Child are by Stuflesser. Extensions of 1968 to the community rooms, also by John Rochford, are skilfully contrived as a bridge over the drive.[1]

The Polish Catholic Centre

A substantial number of Polish immigrants settled in Sheffield after the war. Their first chaplain, Fr Michael Szymankiewicz, resided initially at St Marie's Presbytery. In 1964 he took a property at 520 Ecclesall Road, which still flourishes as the Polish Catholic Centre.

An extension on the garden side of the house was designed in 1967 by John Rochford and Partner. This consists of a hall 42 ft square with clerestory lighting. The hall is adaptable for various uses, having a stage sited across one corner, with a screened section containing an altar. In the entrance are displayed heraldic shields of Polish cities, and a panel commemorating the millennium in 1966 of Polish Christianity. Since 1978 the chaplain's residence has been at 32 Bristol Road.[2]

The Sacred Heart Church

Shortly before St William's mission was founded, Fr Michael Burke was making spiritual provision for the Catholic soldiers of the Artillery Barracks in Langsett Road. Mass had been said for the troops in St Marie's Church, and later in the lower schoolroom of St Vincent's. Having obtained War Office permission, Fr Burke celebrated the first Mass in the barracks chapel on 23rd November 1856. From 1860 civilians were admitted to the services there, and from this beginning sprang the parish of the Sacred Heart. From about the turn of the century, however, civilians were no longer admitted to the barracks chapel. So, as a temporary measure, Fr Joseph Hanley rented a room above a butcher's shop in Langsett Road, where Mass could be said. Then land was bought and in 1903 the Sacred Heart School was erected. One classroom was fitted with a shutter that enclosed a sanctuary, and this room served as a school chapel from 20th July

1. *CBR.N* (1960), p. 127; (1968), pp. 324, 377; Pevsner, p. 477; Cassidy, p. 39.
2. *CBR.N* (1967), pp. 384-85; *Cathedral*, p. 25.

1903. This was initially in the care of Fr Edmund Comerford who served the district from St Vincent's Church.

The Sacred Heart parish was formally instituted in 1920 with the appointment of Fr Robert Dunford. He built a temporary church at a cost of £3,000, which was opened in February 1921. Then Fr Dunford bought the presbytery and another house that provided the site for the present church.

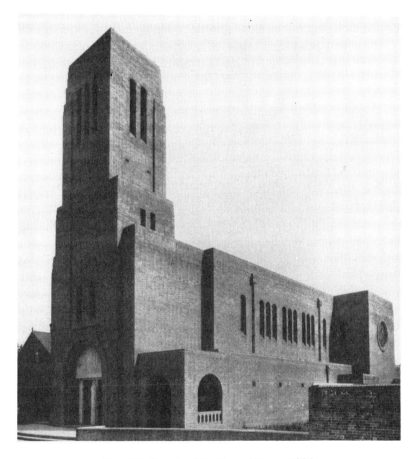

Plate 20 Church of the Sacred Heart, 1936

The church, opened by Archbishop Downey on 25th March 1936, was praised for its artwork as well as for its architecture. The exterior view of tower, nave and transepts, brick-built in a Romanesque-derived modern style, presents a pleasing combination of well-proportioned masses. The Portland stone tympanum and trumeau displaying the Lourdes group and the Sacred Heart at the western entrance were sculpted by Philip Lindsay Clarke.

The interior comprises a west gallery and vestibule, nave and aisles of five bays, transepts, apsidal chancel and two chapels. The handmade Lincolnshire bricks, the glass in plain and yellow hues, and the polished stone flags provide a restrained background for the artwork: the teak doors, pews, and organ case (of 1936 by Albert Keates); the baptismal font of Portland stone and Agba wood; and the Stations of the Cross and St Theresa (of 1936 by Philip Lindsay Clarke). Dominating the interior is the tall mosaic figure of the Sacred Heart with supporting angels in the apse. This, with the Ave Maria and Ave Joseph above the chapel entrances, was executed in 1936 by Eric Newton. The reredos mosaics in geometric patterns within the chapels were added by the same artist in 1961. The statues of Our Lady of Lourdes and St Joseph were sculpted in Portland stone by Philip Lindsay Clarke. St Joseph holds a model of the church in his right hand. The architects of the church were Messrs Hadfield, Cawkwell and Davidson; the builders W.G. Robson Ltd.[1]

The Sacred Heart School

The parish school, part of which was used as a chapel, was opened on 20th July 1903 with an intake of 115 children. Fr Dunford built the temporary church in 1921. Following the opening of the present church in 1936, the temporary church was pressed into service as a parish hall. It has long been used by the school for classroom and canteen purposes. In 1939 on the outbreak of war, 110 children and their teachers were evacuated to Melton Mowbray in Leicestershire. In the blitz in December 1940, the school sustained considerable damage, with roofs and windows broken.

Following their arrival in the parish in 1944, the Sisters of the Poor Child Jesus took up work in the school. In 1979–80, the school build-

1. *Jubilee*, pp. 4-16; *Architectural Review* 80, (1936), pp. 61-62; *SDT* (25 Mar. 1936), p. 4.

ings received a facelift. New toilets were provided for the children and the old area was converted to administration rooms. At the same time, the hall partition was rearranged to provide three clear areas, with quiet rooms adjoining practical rooms and stores. The work cost approximately £54,000 and was planned by the architects John Rochford and Partners.[1]

The Carmelite Monastery of the Holy Ghost

Served by the priests of the Sacred Heart parish is the Carmelite convent at Kirkedge. The Sisters have been there since 1911, but the foundation is older.

As long ago as 1871, plans were in preparation by Hadfield and Son for an orphanage for 300 children. Duke Henry provided eighteen acres of land and paid for the premises. The stone buildings were planned to cover an area of 300 square ft. By 1876, the place is listed in the *Catholic Directory* as an Industrial School for girls, under the care of the Sisters of Charity. A new wing was opened in 1885, comprising a chapel in the Renaissance style 90 ft long by 26 ft wide, dormitory and infirmary. This and the original premises were modelled on the architecture of the Mother House of the Sisters of Charity in the Rue de Bac in Paris. The architects were again Hadfield; the builders were Messrs Tomlinson of Leeds and Sheffield, and the clerk of works was Mr D. O'Neill. The cost of the work was £1,500, and there was now accommodation for 200 girls. To help to defray the cost, Cardinal Manning came to Sheffield to preach at St Marie's church.

After 1887 the orphanage is no longer listed in the *Catholic Directory*. Owing to difficulties over the supply of water, the buildings were abandoned, and the girls were transferred to St Joseph's Home at Walkley. From that time a Catholic society used the buildings as a holiday centre for poor boys from Sheffield. Then about the turn of the century, the premises were used for a few years as a reformatory by the Home Office.

In 1910 the Duke of Norfolk presented the land and building to the Carmelites. About twelve sisters came from Notting Hill Carmel, where the accommodation was overtaxed. But first some £10,000 was

---

1. *Jubilee*, pp. 22-23; *CBR.N* (1980), pp. 100-101.

spent in fitting up the premises. Building extensions designed by Messrs C. and C.M. Hadfield included new parlours and rooms for three lay sisters, and a massive stone wall twelve feet high that enclosed seven acres of the estate. A public chapel seating 150 persons, which forms part of the Carmelite system, was added at this time. Behind a large grille to the left of the sanctuary is the nuns' choir. The convent and chapel were inaugurated by Bishop Cowgill on 16th July 1911.[1]

The Sisters of the Poor Child Jesus

Canon Dunford was desirous of having religious in the Sacred Heart parish. The instrument of the occasion was Fr Vermiere, a Dominican, who put the Provincial of the Order in contact with the Canon. The house in Minto Road was bought on behalf of the Sisters, who moved in and adapted it to their needs. Foundation Day was celebrated on 12th August 1944, with five Sisters present at the first Mass in the convent chapel. Two Sisters became teachers in the parish school and others undertook various works in the parish. From this nucleus, a property adjacent to the convent was acquired in 1947, and the work of the Sisters was extended to the care of needy children. In 1953 another property in Dykes Hall Road at the rear of the convent was acquired, and in 1978 Southbourne, the former home of Dr Birks, was added to the group.

Subsequently the Sisters became fully active in other directions—helping sick and house-bound parishioners, assisting with church music and liturgy, and working within the Catholic Welfare Society of Hallam. At the time of writing, however, their work here is coming to an end, and the Sisters are in the process of leaving the parish. One only will continue to work for the Hallam Diocesan Caring Service.[2]

1. *St Vincent's*; *Jubilee*, p. 24; Hadfield, pp. 169-70; *BR* (1 Apr. 1871), p. 253; *BN* (14 Nov. 1884), p. 782; (17 July 1885), p. 107; (28 July 1911), p. 114; *SDT* (5 July 1910), p. 3); (17 July 1911), p. 11.
  2. *Jubilee*, pp. 24-26.

Chapter 8

FOUNDATIONS EAST:
ST CHARLES; ST JOSEPH; ST MARTIN

Church of St Charles

The mission at Attercliffe was founded from St Marie's on 15th June 1864. On a plot of land at Salmon Pastures, Canon Fisher erected a chapel dedicated to St Catherine, the pre-Reformation patron saint of Sheffield. Its purpose was to serve the east end of the town, whose population was increasing under the stimulus of the expanding steelworks now concentrated there. Initially, the chapel was served from St Marie's, with Mass on Sundays. In 1867–68, the present church of St Charles was built. The freehold site was given by Mr William Wake of Osgathorpe. The Duke of Norfolk gave £500 towards the cost of building, and Mrs Wake and family gave a similar amount. The foundation stone was laid on 3rd December 1867. The architects were Messrs Innocent and Brown of Prior Court, Sheffield, the contractor was John Milner, and the estimated cost was £4,700.[1]

The new church was opened by Dr Cornthwaite, Bishop of Beverley, on 11th August 1868. It was dedicated to St Charles, in memory of the Wakes' eldest son, who had been drowned in January 1867 in an accident on the Serpentine. Only the nave and presbytery were built when the church was first opened. With further help from the Duke of Norfolk and Mr and Mrs Wake, extensions at a cost of

1. Hadfield, p. 140; *Catholic Monthly* (Sept. 1950); *Br* (14 Dec. 1867), p. 914. Both Charles John Innocent (1837–1901) and Thomas Brown had been pupils of Hadfield, Son and Garland. Innocent was President of the Sheffield Society of Architects. Following the Education Act of 1870, he built about twenty schools in and around Sheffield, and in 1874 published *Illustrations of Public Elementary Schools*. He was architect of the Montgomery Hall, Glossop Road Baptist Church and St John's Chapel, Crookesmoor. See *Builders' Journal* (11 Dec. 1901); *Br* (14 Dec. 1901), p. 538.

£2,400 were undertaken by Fr Hurst in 1887. These included the baptistery and two west porches; a prolongation of the nave; and the chancel, Lady chapel and sacristies to the east. The church was reopened on 2nd July 1887 with a High Mass in the presence of Bishop Cornthwaite. The architect of the extensions was C.J. Innocent, and the contractor was John Lister of Aston.

Plate 21 Church of St Charles, 1868

St Charles's Church is built entirely of stone, in the Gothic style, with a front presenting a lofty gable with two two-light traceried windows between which a deep buttress is formed into a canopied niche containing a figure of St Charles. This buttress supports a bell turret above the gable. The church interior consists of western baptistery flanked by two porches, unaisled nave of five bays, and chancel. The nave has a hammerbeam roof, with its principals resting on stone corbels; the side windows consist of two lights with plate tracery. The chancel is two bays deep, with a wide chancel arch, a three-light east window and arch-braced timber roof. The organ to the south is of 1911 by Norman Beard. Beyond a cusped arched screen to the north is the Lady chapel. The substantial oaken pulpit bears Gothic detail. This, with the screens and stalls, was designed by C.J. Innocent and executed by Harry Hems of Exeter. The tile floors were also designed by Innocent, manufactured by Maw and Company, and laid by Mr Potter of Lichfield. The Stations of the Cross are cast relief tableaux with substantial Gothic frames.[1]

The parish school to the east of the church, two-storeyed and of brick, was built in 1871, and rebuilt in 1929 in memory of Fr Joseph Hurst, founder and first rector, 1866–1905, according to a plaque in Heppenstall Lane. The building underwent some structural reorganization in 1964 under the direction of Messrs Hadfield, Cawkwell and Davidson. Owing to diminishing numbers, however, it was closed in 1981.

The school building was then used for three years as a diocesan-sponsored YTS establishment, involving building, catering, computing, crafts, office management, and so on. Between seventy and eighty people at a time were employed there through that period. Subsequently the building was refurbished under the direction of John Rochford and Partners, and opened as the Diocese of Hallam Pastoral Centre. It incorporates now the administration of the diocese, and the public facilities of conference room, library, youth office, resource centre for teachers and adult education centre. The centre was formally opened on 27th June 1990 by Archbishop Luigi Barbarito, the Papal pro-nuncio to Great Britain.[2]

St Joseph's Church, Handsworth

The 'Woodhouse (1868) New Station, served from St Marie's' first appears in the *Catholic Directory* in 1869. From 1867, Mr John Howe had lent a room in which he conducted an afternoon service, until the help of St Marie's clergy was obtained. Then Mass was said at the mission house, near Woodhouse Hall in Stubbin Lane (now Stradbroke Road). A temporary chapel dedicated to St John of Beverley was opened by Canon Walshaw on 9th June 1870. The chapel was of timber, the roof and sides covered with felt, measuring 50 ft by 18 ft,

1. *SRI* (12 Aug. 1868), p. 4; (4 May 1887), p. 2; *The Tablet* (7 May 1887), p. 751.
2. *CBR.N* (1964), p. 428; *The Tablet* (2 Nov. 1872), p. 564; *Hallam News* (Aug. 1990), p. 1.

built by Mr John Turner and Mr J. Greenwood under the direction of Mr Hadfield.

Meanwhile Mgr de Hearne visited Sheffield from Belgium in 1869, and founded an institution for Catholic deaf-mutes in a cottage at Handsworth Woodhouse. Bishop Cornthwaite soon adapted this as a public institution, and appointed Fr Theophilus van Cauwenberghe as chaplain. Shortly afterwards, the Sisters of Charity took charge of the institution, which was recognized by the English bishops in 1874 as serving the whole country. In June 1875, the institution moved from Handsworth Woodhouse to Boston Spa. At the same time Fr van Cauwenberghe, who had been jointly chaplain of the mission and of the institution, moved to Barnsley, and Fr Adrian van Roosmalen became the missionary priest.[1]

During these years, exertions had been made towards building a church in the district. Following a promise of the Duke of Norfolk to Fr Roosmalen, the present church, presbytery and school materialized in 1879–1881. The church foundation stone was laid by Bishop Cornthwaite on 27th August 1879. The design was made by M.E. Hadfield and Son; the builder was Martin Dowling of Harriett Street, Sheffield. The style is the Perpendicular phase of Gothic, following such local churches as Rotherham and Laughton; the materials used were fine red sandstone from the Duke's quarries at Bole Hill, and Broseley tiles. The cost of the church is variously estimated as £6,000–£7,000; the total cost of site, church, presbytery and schools as £8,000–£9,000. The sources are unanimous, however, in reporting that all was completely provided by the Duke of Norfolk. When it was opened on 7th June 1881, the church consisted of nave, north aisle, chancel, north-east Lady chapel and sacristy. The west end of the church was not then complete. The westernmost bay of the nave, the south porch, baptistery and choir gallery were added by Messrs Hadfield, Cawkwell and Davidson in 1956–57. The reopening of the church took place in the presence of Bishop Heenan on 19th March 1957.

The church interior consists of west vestibule and former baptistery beneath the gallery, nave and north aisle of six bays, a deep chancel, north-east Lady chapel and south-east sacristies. There is a crypt beneath the chancel, approached by steps from the north aisle. Perhaps

1. Hadfield, p. 146; *Catholic Monthly* (Sept. 1950); *The Tablet* (25 June 1870), p. 816; *CD* (1869, 1875).

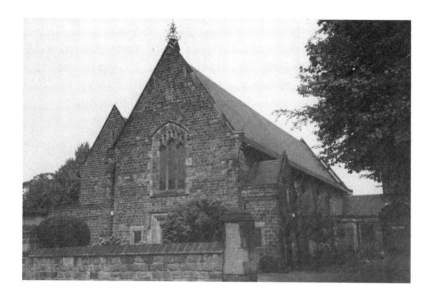

Plate 22 Church of St Joseph, Handsworth, 1881

the most striking feature are the nave piers, octagonal in plan, but taking on at the four cardinal faces pentagonal pilasters which are crenellated beneath the arcade arches. The crenellations were most likely derived by Charles Hadfield from the nave piers of Sheffield Parish Church, now the Anglican Cathedral.

For the rest, all the detailing is conventional neo-Perpendicular—three-light nave windows, wagon roof and tiled floors. The piecemeal installation of furnishings at different times has been tasteful, all blending with the original interior. These include the Stations of the Cross by E. de Fernelmont—large tableaux in high relief, the gift of the Roosmalen family; the font of 1924; the screen separating the chancel and the Lady chapel, 1929; the statue of St Anthony supplied by Burns, Oates and Washbourne, 1932; the marble altar, the stone reredos with figures of St John Fisher and St Thomas More, and the stained glass window in the sanctuary, 1949; the statue of St Theresa,

1940; and the Lady chapel window by Hardman, 1950. Two terra-cotta murals designed by Miss Philippa Threlfall for the new chapel of St John Fisher School were placed on the north wall of the church by Mgr Michael Keegan when the school was closed. When the sanctuary was reordered in 1973, the altar of 1941 was brought forward and the altar rails, pulpit and rood screen were removed.[1] The presbytery, in the same style and materials, together with its spacious garden, forms a pleasing composition with the southern aspect of the church.

The parish school was opened in 1872 and received a new building in 1881, contemporary with the church. Extensions are recorded in 1899, 1925–26, 1936 and 1938, the latest known being in 1971 by Messrs Hadfield, Cawkwell and Davidson. St Joseph's became a primary school in 1965, following the opening of St John Fisher Comprehensive School in Beaver Hill Road, Woodhouse. This three-form entry school, designated to take 450 senior children from the south and east sides of the city, was designed by Messrs Hadfield, Cawkwell and Davidson, and built at a cost of approximately £210,000. When opened in April 1965, it had a four-storey teaching and administration block linked to a single storey wing containing chapel, assembly hall, kitchens and gymnasium; and a separate two-storey practical block housing woodwork, metalwork, housecraft and art rooms. The 13-acre site furnished over nine acres of playing fields. Regrettably, the school was closed in 1981 owing to falling numbers and to the consequent overall reorganization of Catholic comprehensive provision within the city.[2]

Church of St Martin

A thriving chapel of ease to Handsworth flourishes at Swallownest. Since 1938 there have been Mass Centres in various places in the neighbourhood, including Dr O'Brien's house at Woodhouse and the

1. Iris and Chris O'Hara, *St Joseph's Handsworth 1881–1981* (Sheffield: St Joseph's Church, 1981); *BN* (29 Aug. 1879), p. 266; *Br* (6 Sept. 1879), p. 1007; *The Architect* (11 June 1881), p. 407; *The Tablet* (6 Sept. 1879), p. 307; (18 June 1881), p. 1001; *SRI* (10 June 1870), p. 4; (28 Aug. 1879), p. 3; (8 June 1881), p. 3; *SDT* (20 Mar. 1957), p. 5; *HC* (Dec. 1940), p. 4.

2 O'Hara, *op. cit.*; *Cathedral*, pp. 35-36; *HC* (Aug. 1938), p. 10; (Oct. 1938), p. 10; *CBR.N* (1962), p. 316; (1964), pp. 420, 423; (1965), pp. 372-77; *The Tablet* (2 Nov. 1872), p. 564.

Oak Inn, Swallownest. The permanent church hall, dedicated to St Martin de Porres, was erected in 1969 at a contract price of £9,150. This can accommodate over one hundred people for Mass, and can double for social events during the week. The architects were Messrs John Rochford and Partners; the contractors Messrs G. Banks of Attercliffe.

The Marist Sisters have had a convent here since October 1981. The mission had a chaplain from 1976 to 1980 in the person of Fr William Delaney; otherwise it has been served from St Joseph's Church, Handsworth.[1]

1. *HC* (Dec. 1938), p. 8; *CD* (1976–1981); *CBR.N* (1970), pp. 306-309.

Chapter 9

FOUNDATIONS NORTH:
ST CATHERINE; ST PATRICK; ST THOMAS MORE

St Catherine's Church

The mission of St Catherine was founded from St Marie's by Canon Walshaw to serve the Catholics in the developing suburbs of Burngreave and Pitsmoor. The Duke of Norfolk gave the first site in Andover Street, and defrayed the cost of the two-storey building designed to serve as a school and a temporary church. The upper room was fitted out as a chapel measuring about 65 ft by 25 ft; the lower schoolroom accommodated about 250 children. Messrs Hadfield and Son were the architects, and John Pearson was the builder. The school chapel was opened by Bishop Cornthwaite on 8th June 1876.

The adjacent presbytery was completed shortly afterwards, bringing the total cost to £6,650. Fr Luke Burke from Thirsk was appointed priest of the mission. In May 1883, the Sisters of Mercy came to 92 Andover Street to teach in the school. Soon the growing congregation required a larger space for worship. Thus, eight years after the school chapel was opened, a freestanding chapel measuring 90 ft by 30 ft was added on the site, at a cost of £1,100. The foundation stone was laid by Canon Walshaw on 3rd August 1884. Stone-built, to harmonize with the school, it was opened on 23rd November. Hadfields were again the architects, and Frederick Ashforth of Minna Road the contractor. At this time, the Duke of Norfolk gave the site for a permanent church in Burngreave Road. To build the chapel, £800 had been borrowed in 1884, and another £300 for the school requirements in 1894. The remnant of the debt appears to have been cleared from the proceeds of a bazaar held in 1899.[1]

1. Hadfield, pp. 160-61; *SDT* (9 June 1876); *SRI* (10 July 1876), p. 11; (25 Nov. 1884), p. 5; *The Tablet* (9 Aug. 1884), p. 233; (29 Nov. 1884), p. 870;

It fell to Canon White to build the new church and presbytery in Burngreave Road. Bishop Cowgill blessed the foundation stone on 16th July 1925, and presided at the opening on 26th November 1926. The architectural firm of Charles Edward Fox and Son of Halifax provided the design. The contract was for £12,000, and with furnishings totalled £13,000. By this time, Gothic had been virtually superseded by other historical styles which were simpler and cheaper to build. St Catherine's Church is a model of the type of Early Christian basilica that can still be seen in Italy. Of red brick with Portland stone dressings, the church stands prominently at the corner of Burngreave Road and Melrose Road. At the south-west corner it has a Romanesque campanile in four storeys bearing a pyramidal roof. Mosaics of St Theresa and St Catherine flank the west entrance.

Plate 23 St Catherine's Church, 1926

Inside there is a west vestibule or atrium with gallery and a wheel window. The nave and chancel run together in six continuous bays. The black marble columns and Carrara capitals support the round-headed arches and clerestory. The nave ceiling is coffered and the aisle roofs vaulted. The inlay of the chancel apse has a mosaic frieze and a cornice of Connemara marble. Extremely prominent is the baldacchino, supported on four marble columns that carry the canopy bearing a figure of Christ the King; the underside is coffered, and the rear is a mass of Travertine marble with gilded domes. The communion rail, marble with inlaid dyes, runs the width of the church; its balusters of red sandstone are capped with grained Connemara marble. All of the chancel stone work was executed in 1936 by W.H. Fraley of Birmingham; the stalls of Romanesque design were built by L. Conray of Daisy Walk, Sheffield. The altar was consecrated on 23rd October 1936 by Bishop Poskitt.

In the north aisle is the organ, by Bower and Dunn of Sheffield. To the north of the aisle stands a three-bay chapel with a flat ceiling and polygonal baptistery at its west end. This was built as a Memorial chapel by Canon White in 1950.[1]

St Catherine's School

Once St Catherine's church was opened in 1926, the old chapel in Andover Street was pressed into service as part of the school premises. The old school was eventually replaced by a new building in Firshill Crescent. The new site was part of an allotment area newly developed by the council, with houses, shops and flats. The school's teaching accommodation is arranged in an open manner around two internal teaching or play courts of different sizes; the south-facing hall and the dining and teaching areas open on to a further court in the centre.

The character of the buildings is domestic rather than industrial: traditional materials of brick cavity walls and tiled pitched roofs were wisely preferred to prefab systems. The contract let for £110,840 included the building and the games pitch; the architects were Messrs John Rochford and Partners. St Catherine's Junior and Infant School was formally opened by Bishop Wheeler and Bishop Moverley on the 10th July 1974. A Nursery Unit with twenty places was completed in September 1976. Its system of construction and finish was similar to

1. J. White, *St Catherine's Church Sheffield 1876–1936 Jubilee Memento* (Sheffield: St Catherine's Church, 1936); *SDT* (24 Nov. 1926), p. 2; (26 Nov. 1926), p. 9; (26 Oct. 1936), p. 4.

the school's. Messrs Rochford were again the architects and the contract price was £23,456.[1]

The Convent of Mercy

The Sisters of Mercy came in 1883 from the Order's convent in Commercial Road in London's east end, to teach in St Catherine's School. Initially they lived in Andover Street, then moved to Burngreave Road in 1884. The convent at the corner of Abbeyfield Road consisted of an old stuccoed house to which a school was attached in 1908. In 1932 there were additions, harmonizing as far as possible with the old buildings. On the ground floor these consisted of an entrance, vestibule, interview room, cloakrooms, assembly hall, laboratory and classrooms. On the upper floor were the new chapel, sacristy, priest's room and four cells. Below the ground floor were the kitchen and laundry. The chapel consisted of an aisleless nave of four bays with double round-headed windows. The nave was panelled in oak to a height of seven feet. There was a recess for the altar, containing three stained glass windows designed by N.H.J. Westlake. The architects of the addition were Messrs Chapman and Jenkinson.

After 1975 the Convent High School was reorganized as a preparatory school. This was closed in 1979. In September 1982 the convent was transferred to 18 Taptonville Crescent; this house was closed in September 1987. Meanwhile in July 1981 a convent was opened in St Patrick's parish at 16 Swanbourne Road, and extended in 1982.[2]

De La Salle College

As early as 1903 the Catholic body expressed the need for a grammar school for boys in the city. The Sisters of Notre Dame had long provided a Catholic secondary school for girls, but no such school existed for boys, who had to go to non-Catholic secondary schools. At a meeting held in December 1903, Charles Hadfield moved the resolution 'that this meeting is of opinion that immediate steps should be taken to establish a Catholic Grammar School in Sheffield'.

1. *CBR.N* (1972), p. 242; (1974), pp. 80-81, 205; (1977), pp. 164-66.
2. *The Architects' Journal*, 8 June 1932, pp. 772-73; *Catholic Education Council Handbook*, 1960–1988; *Hallam Diocesan Year Book* (1989), p. 61.

A permanent foundation was not made, however, until the 1920s. In 1922 the Brothers of the Christian Schools arrived in Sheffield and took up posts at St Marie's and St Vincent's schools. They were generally referred to as 'the De La Salle Brothers', after the name of the order's founder, St John-Baptist de La Salle (1651–1719). Their first home was the master's house at St Marie's School in Edmund Road. Then the Brothers were established at Osgathorpe Hall in Scott Road (within St Catherine's parish) where they opened De La Salle College, a grammar school for boys, on 11th September 1923. A substantial addition to the original building was opened by Bishop Cowgill on 2nd May 1925, in the presence of the Lord Mayor, the Bishop of Nottingham, Canon Dolan, Philip Wake, KSG, and Brother Benedict, Provincial. There was further building work in 1930 and 1937. Postwar extensions to the original facilities included the conversion of the original hall into a library; the replacement of the old gymnasium, with new facilities adapted from a wartime emergency water tank; and also craft rooms, assembly hall, chapel, laboratories and sixth form rooms.

In the meantime the Brothers had bought Beauchief Hall, a large seventeenth-century house with extensive grounds on the south side of the city, with the aim of building a new school. This plan was disallowed by the authority, and so the hall was rented to a private school, and the grounds were used by the College as sports fields. Then with the advent of secondary reorganization, the College in Scott Road amalgamated with St Paul's School as an 11–18 mixed comprehensive, to be called All Saints. Initially this operated on two sites, but eventually the Brothers sold the Scott Road school, withdrawing from the city, and All Saints was housed entirely in the premises at Granville Road.[1]

St Patrick's Church

St Patrick's parish was founded from St Catherine's. With great foresight, Canon White perceived the missionary potential of a district that was to become the centre of the city's largest building estate.

1. *St Patrick's Sheffield Golden Jubilee 1939–1989* (Sheffield: St Patrick's Church, 1989); *Cathedral*, pp. 18, 35-36; Cassidy, pp. 13, 25-26; *HC* (Apr. 1938), p. 4; *The Tablet* (12 Dec. 1903), pp. 951-54; (9 May 1925), p. 638. *CBR.N* (1963), pp. 336-37; (1968), pp. 310-15; (1973), pp. 152-53.

From 1924, a priest came from St Catherine's to say Mass on Sundays in the Co-op store in Bellhouse Road. At the same time a committee was formed to finance a church and school. Then a ten-acre site in Barnsley Road was purchased by the Canon, and quickly developed: in 1927 the school was built with a hall in which Mass could be said; in 1935 the presbytery; and eventually the permanent church. The parish was formally instituted in 1930, Fr Bernard Ford from Selby becoming the first rector. By 1940 Fr Ford had a parish of 2,000 souls, and a new church with accommodation for 250. The foundation stone was blessed by Bishop Poskitt on 20th June 1939, and the church was opened without formality on the Feast of Corpus Christi, 23rd May 1940. The architect was Robert Cawkwell. Only the chancel, nave and north entrance were then built, at a cost of £4,000, the rest being deferred until after the war. This work was undertaken in 1955, and by February 1956 the church was virtually doubled in size, with the addition of the tower, aisles, organ gallery and Lady chapel, at a cost of £15,000.

Plate 24 St Patrick's School and Church, 1939

Large, tall and brick built, St Patrick's Church was designed in the neo-Early Christian style of St Catherine's, with nave, narrow passage aisles, chancel and prominent north campanile. The church is correctly orientated, so that the eastern apse faces the road, and the west door is furthest away from it. The main entrance is at the foot of the campanile. The church's furnishings are few and tasteful. Notable among them are the two windows in the apse, the large Siena-type crucifix, and the Stations of the Cross, unframed relief carvings.[1]

St Patrick's School

The school opened on 29th August 1927, with approximately one hundred children aged five to fourteen. The rectangular building had four classrooms, with separate cloakrooms for boys and girls on the ground floor, and a staff room and a large hall on the first floor. The hall was additionally used on Sundays (and later on weekdays) as a church. The altar at one end was curtained when not in use.

The perennial overcrowding within the school was somewhat eased in 1954 with the opening of St Thomas More's Primary School at Grenoside. Then matters were further improved from 1958 when the senior pupils and teachers moved to the new St Peter's Secondary Modern School in Morall Road. Following this, St Patrick's was reorganized as a junior and infant school. Eventually certain much-needed improvements and extensions updated the original building. A new wing completed in 1967 provided an assembly-cum-dining hall with kitchens and inside toilets, positioned to form an internal court. Then further work including the remodelling and enlargement of classes and the conversion of the old hall to classrooms was undertaken. This was designed by Messrs Hadfield, Cawkwell and Davidson, at an overall contract price of £21,700. In 1985 one of the classrooms was converted into a 26-place Nursery Unit. This was opened on 6th January 1986 by Bishop Moverley, in the presence of the Lord Mayor and Lady Mayoress. The architect of this work was Anthony Tranmer. In 1971–72 the Anglican Church of Christ the King in Deerlands Avenue was purchased for £9,000 by Fr Michael Daly,

---

1. *St Patrick's School Golden Jubilee* (Sheffield: St Patrick's Church, 1977); Cassidy, p. 16; *HC* (July 1939), pp. 1, 10; (May 1940), pp. 1, 4; *CD* (1926–1990).

and converted into a social centre at a further cost of £17,000.[1]

St Thomas More's Church

St Thomas More's parish was founded from St Patrick's, initially with Sunday Mass in Meynell Road Council School from 1943. Then in 1945 Fr Gallon and Fr Francis Holland, the priest in charge of the mission, acquired a house, 425 Halifax Road. A large room on the first floor served as an additional Mass centre. As the congregation grew, a site on the corner of Halifax Road and Cowper Avenue was bought from the council for £900. Here a multi-purpose church hall was built, and opened as a church by Mgr Canon Hawkswell in June 1950. Known as the church of St Thomas More, this serves as a chapel of ease to the church of the same name in Wordsworth Avenue.

The chapel of ease consists of an unaisled nave of four bays, with the altar recessed in the fifth bay. At the four corners of the building are ancillary rooms beneath the same roof. The construction is of brick and pre-cast reinforced concrete, with a span of 35 ft and a height of 30 ft. The architects were Messrs Hadfield, Cawkwell and Davidson, and the construction was the work of Ferro–Concrete and Stone of Retford. The austere interior is considerably enhanced by the carved crucifix and three saints and the Stations of the Cross donated by parish families. The Crucifix, the Sacred Heart and Our Lady of Fatima were carved by Harry R. Stone, and St Thomas More by Walter V. Cowen.

The initiator of the church and parish centre in Wordsworth Avenue was Fr Thomas O'Reilly. In 1967 he obtained an island site in Margetson Crescent for £1,000 from the council. Here in the centre of the large housing estate of Parson Cross, an original complex comprising church, social centre, meeting rooms, youth club and old persons' club was erected to the design of Anthony Tranmer of John Rochford and Partners. Building began in January 1968, and the centre was officially opened and the church dedicated by Bishop Moverley on 22nd May 1969. The contract price was £74,000, and furnishings cost a further £4,000.

Symbolically, the church stands at the centre of the group, capable of being combined with the social hall that doubles its capacity by

1. *CBR.N* (1964), pp. 420-21; (1968), pp. 306-307.

means of screens and curtains. Constructed of reinforced concrete supports with brick infill, the plan consists of a squarish nave and aisles with rectangular clerestory and ceiling windows, with no structural distinction towards the chancel apart from a narrow central recess in the east wall. Over the altar is a large crucifix, and mounted on the aisle walls two long panels depicting the Way of the Cross, executed in slabs of coloured glass on a white surface by Patrick Feeney of John Hardman Studios. Their arresting semi-abstract effect is further enhanced by the north-east chapel's window which depicts the life of Christ, culminating in the institution of the Blessed Sacrament. The artist executant was Joseph Fisher of Shrigley and Hunt's Studio, Lancaster.[1]

St Thomas More's School; St Peter's School

Meanwhile, the parish primary school had been founded in Creswick Lane in the early fifties. A scheme designating seven classrooms with hall and administration rooms from designs by Messrs Hadfield, Cawkwell and Davidson was begun in April 1953 at a contract price of £33,000. Five months before the agreed date of completion, the school was formally opened by Bishop Heenan on 8th May 1954.

Then came St Peter's Secondary School, designed by the same architects as a three-form entry school for 560 children. The building contract was awarded in December 1956, at a figure of £153,844, the contractors being Messrs George Longden and Sons. The school was formally opened by Bishop Dwyer on 22nd April 1959. Its large complement of secondary children was drawn from various all-age schools—St Patrick's, St Catherine's, the Sacred Heart, St Charles's, St Thomas More's, St Mary's at Mortomley and St Ann's at Stocksbridge.

Built on rising ground, and planned around an internal courtyard, the school offered a commanding view, with playing fields immediately adjacent. The accommodation included a main teaching block three storeys high, hall, gymnasium, administrative block and science wing. The structure was of reinforced concrete with timber curtain

1. *St Thomas More, Sheffield* (Sheffield: St Thomas More Church, 1969); K. Isherwood, 'Church Sculpture', in *The Studio* (Feb. 1952), pp. 44-45; *CBR.N* (1954), p. 51; (1956), p. 129; (1957), p. 87; (1967), pp. 386-87; (1969), pp. 62-67.

walling and brick infill panels. At the request of the diocesan authorities, a permanent chapel with a fixed altar of Ancaster stone was incorporated into the assembly hall.

A two-storey addition including teaching and ancillary rooms was erected in 1974–75 to designs of John H. Black of Huddersfield. However, owing to the reorganization of Catholic secondary education within the city, St Peter's School was closed in 1985.[1]

A Mass centre, served from St Catherine's, was established in the Shirecliffe Estate Primary School in 1941. The Assumption chapel of ease in Herries Road was opened in 1953 and closed at Easter 1986. From 1968 to 1984 this was served from St Marie's.[2]

---

1. Cassidy, p. 17; *St Peter's School, Handbook of Opening* (Sheffield: St Peter's School, 1959); *CBR.N* (1953), p. 132; (1954), p. 176; (1957), p. 308; (1958), p. 330; (1959), pp. 406-407; (1975), pp. 164-65.
   2. *CD* (1954–1986); *Hallam Diocesan Year Book* (1989), p. 29.

Chapter 10

FOUNDATIONS SOUTH:
ST WILFRID; THE MOTHER OF GOD;
THE HOLY FAMILY; OUR LADY AND ST THOMAS;
THE ENGLISH MARTYRS

St Wilfrid's Church

Up to this point, the various missions have been treated in chrono-logical order of their foundation. Thus the preceding chapters have dealt in turn with the churches of St Marie, St Vincent, St William, the Sacred Heart, St Charles, St Joseph and St Catherine, together with their own parochial and missionary foundations. We come now to St Wilfrid's, the last one to be founded in the nineteenth century.

By the 1870s, the Catholics of Sharrow, Heeley and Highfields were in dire need of their own church. Thus a mission was founded for them from St Marie's by Canon Walshaw. Once again, the Duke of Norfolk gave the site, on the corner of Queen's Road and Shoreham Street, and paid for the group of buildings dedicated to St Wilfrid. These buildings, designed by M.E. Hadfield and Son, included school accommodation for 800 boys, girls and infants, and a residence for the master. The boys' school was arranged to serve as a temporary chapel with seating for about 300 worshippers. The scheme also included the provision of land for a permanent church and presbytery, which however never materialized on this site.

High Mass was celebrated in the school chapel on 15th October 1879 by Bishop Cornthwaite, no longer Bishop of Beverley, but appearing in Sheffield for the first time as Bishop of Leeds. The schools were blessed and opened on 23rd November by Fr Julius de Baere, whom the Bishop placed in charge of the mission.

The air raids of 12th-13th December 1940 caused such serious damage to the buildings that the only portion usable thereafter was the church. The presbytery, though damaged, was not wrecked, and here

Fr Dunleavy had a temporary weekday chapel. The Abbeydale Cinema and the chapel of St Elizabeth's Home in Heeley Bank Road also saw service as temporary venues for Sunday Mass. Then Fr Dunleavy bought the house at 9 Machon Bank Road, with a view to the possible re-siting of the nucleus of the parish. This house now served as the presbytery and a daily Mass centre. Eventually the church in Queen's Road was rehabilitated, and this was boosted by additional services at Abbeydale School, at Arbourthorne Council School (1946), and then in St Peter's Church of England schoolroom in Machon Bank. Following the acquisition of the house in Machon Bank Road, the old presbytery at 524 Queen's Road fell into disrepair. However, it was extensively restored in 1989. From 1990 under the name of St Wilfrid's Centre, it housed the Hallam Diocesan Caring Service and the Catholic Marriage Advisory Council.[1]

Plate 25 St Wilfrid's Church, 1879

1. Hadfield, p. 168; SRI (16 Oct. 1879), p. 2; *Cathedral*, p. 13; *Catholic Monthly* (Sept. 1950); *Hallam News* (July 1990), p. 5.

The Church of the Mother of God

11th June 1952 was a happy day for Fr Dunleavy, when Bishop Heenan blessed the Church of the Mother of God. The first Abbeydale Congregational Church (which still stands) was built in 1884 to designs of William Hemsoll and Joseph Smith, architects of Sheffield. This proving inadequate, a larger church was built next to it in 1901. On account of its dwindling congregation, however, this was sold in 1952 to Mr G. Brookes of Thryberg as a store room. When this became uneconomical, the owner sold the building to the Catholics of St Wilfrid's parish for use as a church.

The church retains its original architectural character, despite extensive alterations for Catholic use. The main front, prominently sited at the corner of Abbeydale Road and St Ronan's Road, exhibits its Nonconformist origins with a strictly symmetrical free Gothic design, the central nave flanked by matching polygonal features. This transeptal arrangement contains staircases to the west gallery, and between them a large vestibule.

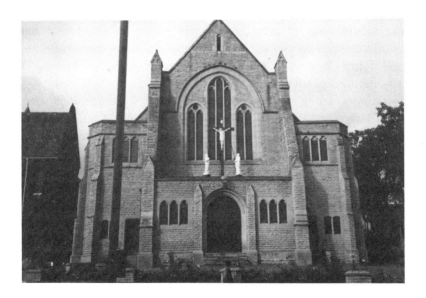

Plate 26 Church of the Mother of God, 1957

Extensive internal reordering by John Rochford and Partners in the 1980s adapted the interior to Catholic use, without destroying its original character. It now consists of a wide unaisled nave-cum-chancel with large west gallery. The chancel arch was blocked, and the former sanctuary converted to a day chapel. The two-sided tabernacle within a glazed strip between the sanctuary and the new chapel serves both altars. Two new floors above the day chapel afford useful ancillary accommodation. The Stations of the Cross in round-headed frames are cast in low relief, and the organ, by Albert Keates, dates from 1892.[1]

St Wilfrid's School

Bombed out of its Queen's Road building in 1940, St Wilfrid's School had a variety of makeshift premises, including the former Vestry Hall in Meersbrook Park Road. Eventually, St Wilfrid's new school in Millhouses Lane was begun in 1955, the first post-war Catholic school to be built within the administrative area of the Sheffield Education Committee. The site on former allotment gardens was surrounded by residential property, with access from Millhouses Lane, Hastings Road and Kingsley Park Avenue.

The school was planned by Messrs Hadfield, Cawkwell and Davidson on three levels, with the hall, kitchen, infant classrooms and Head's room on the entrance level between upper and lower junior floors, taking advantage thereby of the sloping site. A variety of materials, including rock-faced random stone walling and pitched roofs of larger precast slates, impart a traditional character in keeping with the location. The school was opened on 16th April 1956.[2]

Church of the Holy Family

The parish of the Holy Family was founded in 1953, having sprung from a Mass centre served from St Wilfrid's since 1944. The buildings at present consist of the presbytery in Eastern Drive and the adjacent dual purpose church-cum-parish hall. This is a plain rectangular brick building with tall windows, and a flat-roofed western

1. J.E. Vickers, *100 Years of Worship 1883–1983*; *CBR.N* (1980), p. 31; *Sheffield Telegraph* (12 June 1952), p. 3; *Church Building* (Easter 1984), p. 59.
2. *CBR.N.* (1954), p. 176; (1956), pp. 213, 218-19.

extension. The interior has facilities for screening off the chancel at the (ritual) east end, and a stage at the west end. The congregational space between is a simple unaisled nave of four bays, with rectangular windows and a shallow pointed, panelled ceiling.

Plate 27 Church of the Holy Family, 1956

Apart from the Stations of the Cross—coloured prints set in wooden frames—there are as yet no furnishings of note. The stage is double-screened, with an extension convertible to a meeting room. There are more ancillary rooms to the south west, and the sacristy to the south east. The architects were Messrs Oxley and Bussey of Pinstone Street.[1]

Following the death of Fr O'Hagan in February 1990, pastoral service was provided by the Presentation Sisters, working in conjunction with the Marist Fathers of St Oswald's parish.[2]

1. *Hallam Diocesan Year Book* (1989), p. 30.
2. *Hallam News* (March 1990), p. 2; (July 1990), p. 2.

Church of Our Lady and St Thomas

Following a meeting of Woodseats Catholics in May 1908, an approach was made to Bishop Brindle of Nottingham, in whose diocese the district then was, expressing the desire for a church. The present site was obtained, and was paid for by Bishop Brindle. A temporary church dedicated to Our Lady of Beauchief and St Thomas of Canterbury was opened by the priest in charge, in the presence of Bishop Brindle, on 16th June 1910. The temporary church cost £400 and seated 250 people. Subsequently it became the parish hall.

The present church was erected during the rectorate of Fr James Rooney. Its foundation stone was blessed by Bishop Dunn on 26th March 1931, and the church was opened on 1st June 1932. The architect was Adrian Gilbert Scott, and the builders Messrs M.J. Gleeson Ltd. The historic style is Italian Romanesque; the plan is conceived as a Greek cross, yielding chancel, transepts and the nave slightly elongated. A square tower, glazed, rises over the crossing. Many of the round-headed windows are subdivided in their lower parts into two or three lights, also round-headed. The planning takes a really sophisticated turn at the crossing, where the re-entrant angles are chamfered, and tunnel vaults raised upon stone columns with Romanesque capitals project from the chamfers. Within the four chamfers are built-in confessionals, the baptistery and the sacristy entrance.

The chancel was re-ordered in 1968; its floor level was lowered and a new forward altar of Ancaster stone installed. The Ancaster stone recovered from the old altar was pressed into service for the lectern and the tabernacle stand. The architects were Messrs John Rochford and Partner.

Several art works were also added in the sixties: three mosaics of the Ascension, the Madonna and Child, and the Sacred Heart, designed by Mayor-Morton and executed by Geoffrey Wheeler (1960–62); silver and wrought iron and copper work from Maria Laach Abbey; the Stations of the Cross by Imogen Stuart of Dublin (1961); the processional cross by Dunstan Pruden; and finally the organ (1989) by Copeman Hunt.

Plate 28 Church of Our Lady and St Thomas, 1932

Sacristies were added to the church in 1959–60 at a cost of £5,600. In 1973–74 new parish rooms linking the church and the hall were erected at a contract figure of £27,500. The building (double glazed towards the A61) blends well with the church, but no attempt was made by the architect (D. Wilkinson of John Rochford and Partners) to imitate Adrian Scott's Lombard Romanesque. The builders were Messrs J.W. Anson and Sons.[1]

1. Wilf Taaffe, *Our Lady and St Thomas, Sheffield 1932–1982*; *CBR.N* (1968), p. 92; (1973), pp. 122-23; (1974), pp. 110, 201; *Hallam Diocesan Year Book* (1989), p. 61. The church hall of 1910 was demolished and replaced by a new parish hall in 1986; the architect was Douglas Wilkinson and the cost was £130,000. Information of Mr. W. Taaffe. *Telegraph and Star* (19 Nov. 1971), p. 13; *SDT* (2 June 1932), p. 12.

The School

St Thomas of Canterbury Primary School in Chancet Wood Road was completed in January 1971. It was formally opened by the Lord Mayor, Alderman Harold Hebblethwaite, and blessed by Bishop Ellis on 18th November. At that date it had 176 children on its roll, drawn from as far afield as Coal Aston and Dronfield. Open arrangements of the teaching areas were devised within a traditional brick-built and tile-roofed structure. The school was designed by Messrs John Rochford and Partners.

From their house at Minto Road, the Sisters of the Poor Child Jesus made a new foundation at 5 Linden Avenue on 14th May 1975.[1]

The English Martyrs Chapel

A Mass Centre served from Our Lady and St Thomas was established at Totley in the Cross Scythes Hotel in 1956. In 1966 a chapel of ease dedicated to the English Martyrs was opened on a site at the corner of Baslow Road and The Crescent. There is space for a permanent church and presbytery, at which juncture the present chapel would become a parish hall.

The chapel, designed by John Rochford, is of square plan, brick-built with a steeply pitched pyramidal slate roof and clerestory. Internally, the square plan is diagonalized respecting the arrangements—i.e. the altar is in the north corner, with the entrance, confessional and ancillary rooms opposite in the south. The altar is of black marble. The Stations of the Cross contain brightly coloured ceramic figures in low relief set in rectangular ceramic frames. The Crucifix is by Arthur Dooley. The main contractors for the chapel were Messrs Bailey and Martyn Ltd.[2]

1. *CBR.N* (1972), p. 166.
2. *Hallam Diocesan Year Book* (1989), p. 29; *CBR.N* (1963), pp. 148-49.

Plate 29 Church of the English Martyrs, 1964

Chapter 11

FOUNDATIONS SOUTH EAST:
ST THERESA; ST OSWALD; OUR LADY OF LOURDES; ST ANTHONY

St Theresa's Church and School

Owing to the development of new housing by the council, the provision of a church and school on the Manor Estate became a necessity in the 1920s. Canon Dolan undertook the arduous duty of making these foundations. From 23rd August 1925, Mass was said on the Manor in an old army hut. By 1927, a regular Sunday Mass was said at 9 a.m. in the Council School. In the meantime, Canon Dolan vigorously campaigned for funds to build a school to be dedicated to St Theresa. One of the Canon's fund-raising ploys was to circularize people listed in the *Catholic Who's Who*. His handbill showed Old Mother Hubbard surveying a cupboard; nearby a dog wearing a biretta was begging. This brought in a substantial sum, and in return the Canon sent each donor a holy picture of St Theresa with a 'thank you' message printed on the back.

Land was bought from the council for £2,000, and the contract to build a school for 400 children was given to J. Hawkins of Heckmondwike. The foundation stone was blessed by Bishop Cowgill on 24th June 1928. The official opening by Cardinal Bourne took place on 4th October 1929, but owing to the prolonged building work, the children did not move in until 7th January 1930. Mass was said in the school hall from October 1929. But the need for a separate church was strongly felt, and this Fr Grogan provided in the thirties. What is now the parish hall, a plain rectangular building with a timber barrel vault and ancillary rooms at the entrance and the rear, was formally opened on 31st May 1938. Messrs Gleeson were the contractors and the cost was £3,000.

ST. THERESA'S NEW SCHOOL,
MANOR ESTATE.

The Cost, £12,000.   Wanted, £8,000.

Could You Spare a Poor Dog a Bone?
DON'T SAY
The Cupboard is Bare.
LOOK AGAIN.   I THINK
THE   LITTLE   FLOWER
Has put something there for me.   We are in desperate need of Help and grateful for any donation however small.

We Offer Holy Mass every week for Benefactors.

CANON DOLAN,
ST. MARIES',
SHEFFIELD.

SIR W. C. LENG & CO. (SHEFFIELD TELEGRAPH), LTD., ALDINE COURT.

Plate 30 Handbill, St Theresa's School, 1920s

Owing to the intervention of the war, St Theresa's permanent church was not erected for another twenty years. Here, the guiding hand was Fr McGillicuddy, the architect John Rochford, and the builders Messrs D. O'Neill and Son. Mr Rochford's first design was costed at £60,000, but this had to be cut to £45,000. The foundation stone was blessed by Bishop Dwyer on 29th June 1958, and the new church was opened in July 1960.

The church was sited some distance from the main road, on a sloping site which allowed for a terraced approach. The slope was retained in the nave, allowing good visibility of the chancel. The opportunity was also taken in planning to connect the sacristy to the existing presbytery by means of a corridor.

The style of the church is non-historical. The external appearance has a strong emphasis on geometrical forms, the parts tastefully arranged. The exterior is tall and well accented, with transverse segmental gables to the nave. The structure is based upon a reinforced concrete frame clad with brick and stone. Above the east end rises a copper-covered dome, standing upon a drum with twelve pilasters sculpted by A. and S. Rochford bearing figures of the Apostles. Balancing this, a lower cylindrical tower contains the west entrance, and above it is the statue of St Theresa by Lindsay Clark.

Plate 31 St Theresa's Church, 1960

The spacious interior consists of a wide nave of seven bays with a tall clerestory, flanked by low aisles which contain built-in confessionals and side chapels. The circular baptistery projects to the south west. Within the west tower is a choir gallery, and an organ by J.W. Walker and Son, dating from 1960. The chancel terminates in an apse that rises taller than the nave into the clerestoried and domed east tower. It is flanked by north and south chapels of St Theresa and Our Lady. The statue of Christ the King above the altar is by Michael Clark; the Stations of the Cross consisting of square blocks bonded to the walls, their detail restrained in low relief, are by Lindsay Clark. The four wooden statues of the Madonna and Child, St Theresa, the Sacred Heart and St Joseph were carved by Lindsay Clark and painted by Michael Clark.

Following the building of St John Fisher Comprehensive School at Handsworth, St Theresa's all-age school was reorganized to take only, juniors and infants. A redevelopment scheme was initiated in 1964 to provide a new infant block, together with a new kitchen and dining facilities. John Rochford was again the architect, and the contract on a tender of £22,556. 10s. 4d was awarded to Messrs J.F. Finnegan and Company Ltd. This work was completed in July 1965.[1]

St Oswald's Church and School

Almost contemporary with St Theresa's parish, another mission was developing on the adjacent Wybourn Estate. Initially, Sunday Mass was said in 1935 in the Catholic chapel of City Road Cemetery, and later in the hall of the Council School. Land was bought for a church to be dedicated in memory of Canon Dolan to his patron, St Oswald, a seventh-century king of Northumbria who was martyred in defence of his kingdom and his faith. The school came first, its foundation stone blessed by Fr Bradley and laid by Brian O'Hara, an infant pupil, on Easter Day, 1939. It was officially opened on 25th April 1940, and here Mass was said until the permanent church was built. This missionary foundation was separated from St Marie's and designated a

---

1. *Souvenir of the Solemn Opening of St Theresa's New Church, Sheffield* (Sheffield: St Theresa's Church, 1960); *HC* (June 1938), p. 1; (Dec. 1938), p. 5; *Catholic Monthly* (Sept. 1950); *Cathedral*, pp. 19-21; *CBR.N* (1959), pp. 142-44; (1964), pp. 427-28; (1965), pp. 379-80.

separate parish in 1948. Fr Gerard Palframan then moved from St Marie's presbytery to his quarters at 386 City Road.

The church was probably the first in the world to be dedicated to Our Lady Queen of Heaven, a new feast proclaimed by the Pope in 1955. It was officially opened by Bishop Heenan on 3rd June in that year. The design was by the architect R.A. Ronchetti of Halifax. The church seats 375 worshippers and cost £17,000. The presbytery was built at the same time.

Lying adjacent to the school, the church has a long nave and a short, lower chancel. It is constructed of multi-coloured sand-faced bricks relieved by stone dressings, and roofed with tiles. Above the west entrance facing Southend Road is a three-light segmental-headed window. Immediately within are an inner porch, baptistery, cloakrooms and stairs to the choir loft. The nave, unaisled and of four bays, has segmental-headed windows, buff-coloured sand-faced brick walls and a panelled, coved ceiling.

Plate 32 St Oswald's Church, 1955

The chancel arch is also segmental, and its jambs tilted inwards. The sanctuary floor, altar rails and steps are in mosaic, the work and the gift of a local Catholic builder. All the furnishings were given by the parishioners. Especially fine is the large free-standing circular domed tabernacle, with its enamelled figures of Christ the King and the Evangelists. The dedication of the church was restored to St Oswald in 1985.[1]

Our Lady of Lourdes Church

After the war ended in 1945, new housing south of the Manor generated estates at Hackenthorpe and Gleadless. From these grew eventually the churches of Our Lady of Lourdes and St Anthony. The Diocesan Year Book records under Hackenthorpe that a Mass centre was established at the Birley Hotel in 1952. The mission was served initially from St Theresa's Church. It had its own priest in the person of Fr Peter McDonagh, who lived at St Theresa's presbytery from 1952, and at 39 Delves Road from 1955. The mission was designated a parish in 1954, and by 1957 Fr McDonagh had the church of Our Lady of Lourdes built and opened.

The church, presbytery and school are grouped in Springwater Avenue on a large site which also contains a playground and playing fields. The spacious church, designed by Messrs Reynolds and Scott of Manchester, while modern in style, bears details which echo the late Gothic tradition. It is constructed of brick with golden rustic facings, with stone dressings to the doors and windows. Planned to seat 400 worshippers, its approximate cost including fittings was £33,700.

The compact exterior, composed of nicely balanced masses, exhibits a long nave (six bays) with low aisles, two south porches, shallow transepts, polygonal chancel and a sturdy west tower supported by octagonal turrets. Within the tower, the west gallery houses the organ by J.W. Walker.

1. *HC* (May 1949), p. 3; (Nov. 1939), p. 4; (Apr. 1940), p. 1; (May 1940), p. 1; *Cathedral*, pp. 21, 24; *Catholic Monthly* (Sept. 1950); *CBR.N* (1954), pp. 103-104; *Sheffield Telegraph* (2 June 1955), p. 2.

Plate 33 Church of Our Lady of Lourdes, 1957

Inside, the height of the nave is further emphasized by the low, narrow aisles, reduced to the width of access passages. The nave is spanned by a series of four-centred reinforced concrete arches, which echo the ribs of mediaeval vault construction. Within the transverse arches of the nave are pairs of tall clerestory windows with multi-coloured panes displaying sacred symbolism.

In 1973 the sanctuary was reordered by Messrs John Rochford and Partner. The principal change was the introduction of a new, elevated sanctuary in front of the old one, nearer and more easily visible to the congregation. The new high altar is of Ancaster stone, and the sedilia of carved oak. The original altar rails of marble and wrought iron were modified, the four chancel steps were covered with terrazzo tiles, and the original font was brought to the lowest step. At the same time, the grilles of six side chapels were removed, and their altars converted to pedestals for statues. To the east, the former sanctuary with its mosaic floor is now the Blessed Sacrament chapel. The original tabernacle stands on a pillar of Ancaster stone; and above it is the original baldacchino with the Dove of Peace. There are shrines of the Sacred Heart, Our Lady of Lourdes and St Bernadette. The Stations of the Cross are wooden tableaux, frameless and carved in low relief.

The St John Fisher Primary School stands to the west of the church. The design, also by Reynolds and Scott, includes a large assembly hall with stage, capable of use as dining space. The school cost £38,000, and was formally opened on 2nd September 1957.[1]

Chapel of Christ the King

When founded in 1952, Hackenthorpe parish included the districts of Beighton and Frecheville. Much older than Hackenthorpe, however, is the mission of Beighton, where a beginning was made from Spinkhill in 1923 by Fr James Nicholson, SJ. After initial house Masses, the congregation opened St Gabriel's Hall off Drake House Lane in 1924. In 1946 the hall was moved by the parishioners to a more central situation in Manvers Square, under the direction of Fr Laurence Cardwell, SJ, and renamed the Chapel of Christ the King. Bishop Moverley visited Beighton in July 1984 to celebrate with the parishioners the Diamond Jubilee of the chapel's foundation.[2]

St Anthony's Church

St Anthony's church hall is the first instalment of a complex of church, hall, school and presbytery. It was completed in the autumn of 1963 at an approximate cost of £20,000, and was opened as a chapel of ease to Our Lady of Lourdes church at Hackenthorpe. It was transferred to St Theresa's parish in 1964. The hall, school and presbytery were never built, and since the need for them is no more, the land has been sold for housing.

Prominently situated on its generous site in Sandby Drive, the church hall was designed by Messrs Reynolds and Scott. The large square hall seats 320 worshippers. The structure, of transverse portal frames of laminated timber, forms a nave of four bays, with panelled

1. *Hallam Diocesan Year Book* (1989), p. 31; *CBR.N* (1957), pp. 179-81, 308-309; *CBR.S* (1973), pp. 108-109.
2. *Catholic Voice* (June 1984), p. 2.

ceiling and rectangular clerestory windows. The altar recess on the south side is capable of being screened during secular functions; it has sacristies on either side. Opposite are ancillary rooms, and here the central north porch was converted to a meeting room by Patrick Cassidy in 1985. At the same time, a new porch was constructed at the north-east corner.[1]

1. *CBR.N* (1963), pp. 150-51; *Hallam Diocesan Year Book* (1989), p. 28; *CD* (1982–1989).

Chapter 12

POST-VATICAN II FOUNDATIONS:
HALLAM DIOCESE; ST MARIE'S CATHEDRAL;
ST FRANCIS

Hallam Diocese

From the end of the war in 1945, it was widely thought that the Leeds diocese was too large for administrative comfort. Following Bishop Heenan's appointment of Mgr Canon John Dinn to the rectorate of St Marie's Church, it seemed to many people that the formation of a new diocese with Sheffield at its head was imminent. However, no change took place for some years. Then in 1968 Bishop Wheeler consecrated the Right Reverend Gerald Moverley, JCD, as Bishop of Tinisa and Auxiliary in Leeds.

Bishop Moverley took up residence in Sheffield, and thenceforth undertook the pastoral care of the southern part of the Leeds diocese. The arrangement was formalized on his translation to the newly erected see of Hallam on 30th May 1980. The new diocese was formed by the division of the dioceses of Leeds and Nottingham, and consists of the County of South Yorkshire, parts of the High Peak and Chesterfield districts of Derbyshire, and the district of Bassetlaw in Nottinghamshire. Fittingly, St Marie's became the cathedral of the new Diocese of Hallam. Fr John Metcalfe served as secretary to Bishop Moverley from 1980. He was succeeded in 1986 by Mgr David Kirkwood.[1]

St Marie's Cathedral

Meanwhile, there had been important developments at St Marie's

---

1. *Cathedral*, pp. 37-38; *Hallam Diocesan Year Book* (1989), p. 9; *CD* (1981, 1987).

which should be noted at this point, for in 1970–72 the whole of the church interior was extensively remodelled.

New benches had already been given by Mr Bernard O'Neill; new communion rails in precast terrazzo by Messrs Hodkin and Jones, and an internal portico with Renaissance features had been installed during the rectorship of Mgr Dinn. Then under the administration of Mgr Sullivan the church was refurbished with two objectives in mind: the first being to adapt the sanctuary to the new forms of the liturgy, following the Second Vatican Council; the second being to do so in a manner in no way detracting from the style and effect of the original architect. First, however, there was a three-year period of thought, consultation and experiment. During this time a full photographic record was made of the church before any permanent alterations took place. Only then were Messrs J.J. Frame and Son of Horsham employed for the work of restoration and renovation.

The alterations entailed the removal of the communion rails and the rood screen, and in doing so the beauty of the east window was revealed in all its glory. The choir stalls in the sanctuary were removed, allowing enormous space for liturgical movement. None of them was in any way wasted, however, for all were made into prie-dieu and episcopal sedilia.

The original altar had been taken down and its successor dedicated as a War Memorial in 1921. Now a new altar was installed towards the front of the sanctuary, and consecrated on 8th September 1972 by Bishop Wheeler and Bishop Moverley. So that the original effect should not be lost, and that there should not be two altars on the sanctuary, the second altar mensa of 1921 was taken away, and the frontal was recessed flush with the reredos. The relics which had been in the first and second altars now repose in the third one.

The nave pulpit was dismantled but not destroyed, for it was used to make a new chancel lectern and a portable font. The church was decorated also, the arch mouldings and the capitals newly highlighted in colour. After insulation, the nave ceiling was adorned with the names and arms of English and Welsh martyrs. In addition, the catafalque over the tomb in the sanctuary was taken down, and the figure of Fr Pratt moved from where he is buried to a place beneath the Mortuary chapel altar. This allowed a ready access to the Blessed Sacrament chapel. Finally, the exterior of the church was sandblasted.

There were further developments in preparing to celebrate the centenary of the consecration of the church in 1989. A damp course was put in, and the whole of the interior was redecorated and rewired. The stone font was moved from the baptistery to a place in the north transept before the Blessed Sacrament chapel. This allowed for baptism to be seen by all the people, especially when the sacrament is conferred during Mass. The opportunity was taken to remove the old timber confessionals and to convert the former baptistery into two soundproof reconciliation rooms or confessionals. The wrought-iron screen which had stood between the baptistery and the nave was now moved to a place between the chancel and the Blessed Sacrament chapel. It was in fact returning to its original place, from which it had to be removed when the organ was installed in 1875.

All of the alterations outlined above contributed to one ultimate end—a place in which the new liturgy may be celebrated conveniently and effectively. At the same time, it is true to say that the beauty of the original building is there for all to see.[1]

Church of St Francis of Assisi

While the foregoing events were in train, the formation of a new Mass centre at Crosspool was taking place, culminating in the erection of the new parish and church of St Francis, Sandygate.

The increasing population in Sheffield's western suburbs of Fulwood, Crosspool and Lodge Moor indicated the post-war need for a new Catholic church. Following the completion of the Notre Dame convent chapel, Mass was said there on Sundays. Then Mgr Dinn acquired premises in Benty Lane, Crosspool, which he opened as a Mass centre. The church of St Francis had been built about 1830 as a school. In the course of its long career the building had also served as a wartime food office, as a library and as the cradle of the Anglican parish of St Columba. The rectangular, stone-built church was four bays long with straight-headed windows and a gable over the centre of its long side. It accommodated about 150 worshippers. This became an independent parish in 1968, in the charge of Fr Ronald Fox. About this time, the church acquired a porch at its west end, which led to the parish centre, constructed in 1978 in part of the former school playground.

1. *CBR.N* (1956), p. 139; (1972), p. 135; *The Tablet* (9 July 1921), p. 60; *Cathedral*, pp. 33, 38.

It was clear, however, that this building was insufficiently large to serve as a permanent parish church. In the 1970s there was a scheme to build a church at Lodge Moor. A site was obtained in Crimicar Lane, and held for some years. Then in 1986 it was decided to erect a church on land donated by Miss Marion Young, next to her home in Sandygate Road. A technical committee of the Parish Council was formed which included a surveyor, a contracts manager, financial officer and an advisor on art works. Three architects were interviewed, and the brief was given to Mr Vincente Stienlet, for the committee had been especially impressed by Mr Stienlet's work on the new church of St Joseph at Wetherby.

The contract was signed with the builders, Messrs John Dixon and Company of Doncaster, on 24th October 1988. Miss Young removed the first turf on 30th October and the foundation stone was blessed on 25th February 1989 by Bishop Moverley, who consecrated and opened the new church on 1st December that year.

This is a truly remarkable design, which well repays a visit. To overcome the difficulties of a restricted site, the church, hall and presbytery are all contrived together, within a hexagonal plan. The complex includes presbytery, church, east entrance, day chapel, sacristies, meeting room and a hall separated from the church by a moveable screen. The complete building is a triumph of thoughtful planning, each component flowing freely into adjacent spaces, and all of them mercifully free from the tyranny of right angles. The day chapel, for instance, is visible from the church through its glazed screen; together, church and chapel form a hexagon within the main complex. The hexagon of the overall plan continues to reappear in the details, as in the floor tiles, and in the base of the baptismal font (by Morag Gordon). The interior is clearly dominated, however, by the carving of the Risen Christ (by Fenwick Lawson) high above the chancel.

Other artworks specially created for the opening of the church include the Stations of the Cross by Maggie Bakkevold; the Processional Cross by Michael Lloyd and Russ Conway; the Icon of Our Lady by Sr Ethna, OSB; St Francis with the Animals by Adrian Peters; the Tapestry of Pope John Paul II and the Banner of St Francis by Esther Lenton; and the Tapestry of the Madonna and Child by Christina Finnigan.

Claremont Hospital, which moved to Sandygate Road in 1953, has had Fr Killeen as its chaplain since 1982. Also in the parish is a house of the Canonesses of St Augustine, founded at 23 Cairns Road in 1975.[1]

Plate 34 Church of St Francis, 1989

1. *Hallam Catholic Voice* (Dec. 1988), p. 4; (Apr. 1989), p. 7; *The Star* (5 Oct. 1989), p. 5; *St Francis of Assisi, Sandygate, Ceremony of Consecration* (Sheffield: St Francis Church, 1989); *Hallam News* (Oct. 1989), p. 6; *Hallam Diocesan Year Book* (1989), pp. 29, 61.

CONCLUSION

As the priest and parishioners of St Francis's Church face the challenges of the nineties, they may feel fortified by the proud traditions that have written the Catholic history of Sheffield; for the case of St Francis is typical of the pattern of missionary development that has operated throughout the land for two centuries.

The customary process of a priest founding a mission where the need is felt by taking a house and opening a chapel, then building a school or school chapel, and finally building a permanent church as and when funds have allowed, has been observed in operation many times in the preceding chapters. A study of the Catholic history of England would reveal the same process at work hundreds of times over, with only slight variations in the details.

Within our survey of this process in Sheffield, the foremost tribute must surely be paid to the sterling work of the clergy in serving local Catholics by means of their sacred calling. I have tried in the following appendix to list every priest who has worked here, together with his years of service. Particularly demonstrative of clerical devotion were the long records of Fr Richard Rimmer at The Lord's House and the New Chapel (42 years); of Fr Adrian van Roosmalen at St Joseph's, Handsworth (47 years); and of Fr George Bradley at St Wilfrid's (48 years). Mention should also be made at this point of Brother William Smith, CM, who at the time of writing has been sacristan of St Vincent's Church for a remarkable 61 years.

Religious Sisters and Brothers also have afforded faithful service through the care of the sick, of the elderly and of needy children. As early as 1604, there were no less than six recusant schoolmasters known in the town. Since this daring commencement, religious and lay teachers in their hundreds have by now served the cause of Catholic education.

Other layfolk have supplied their talents generously in the sphere of parochial development—architects, artists, builders and decorators.

The weekly round of liturgical administration is assisted also by devoted altar servers, musicians, readers, collectors, bellringers, cleaners and the rest who give of their time as well as their talents.

In the sphere of patronage, a prominent role has long been played by the Dukes of Norfolk. In allowing their agents to open the domestic chapel in The Lord's House to local Catholics, they sustained the mission continuously. The task of listing all of the many benefactions to the cause of religion in Sheffield and elsewhere by successive Dukes and members of their family we must leave to another hand. Suffice it to say that sites, schools, churches and furnishings in abundance have prospered immeasurably through their generosity.

Other patrons there were, however, and well remembered in Sheffield are the family names of Bernasconi, Broomhead, Ellison, Eyre, Hadfield, Knight, Munster, Revell, Sutton, Wake, Wright and Young. Together with these must be acknowledged those many unnamed poor members of congregations, whose pennies and shillings have made them also benefactors of the Church.

It would be perverse to dismiss all this service as valueless or even merely incidental. Rather should this giving of talents be interpreted as a continuous affirmation of people's religious faith. May this continuity of effort that springs from faith and centres on the Lord's house long continue past the nineties and into the millennium.

APPENDIX

Rectors and Administrators of St Marie's Cathedral Church

1850–1855	Rev. Edmund Scully
1855–1866	Rev. William Fisher
1866–1896	Rev. Samuel Walshaw
1896–1898	Rev. James Gordon
1898–1935	Rev. Oswald Dolan
1935–1936	Rev. Thomas Bentley
1936–1951	Rev. James Bradley
1951–1964	Rev. John Dinn
1965–1968	Rev. George Collins
1968–1985	Rev. Stephen Sullivan
1985–	Rev. John Ryan

Assistant Priests

1843–1850	Rev. Matthew Kavanagh
1849–1850	Rev. Thomas Lynch
1850–1858	Rev. Joseph Hill
1852–1859	Rev. Francis Callibert
1854–1855	Rev. Edward Gosford
1858–1860	Rev. William Pope
1859–1860	Rev. John Hill
1859–1863	Rev. Thomas Loughran
1859–1865	Rev. Patrick Kennedy
1860–1864	Rev. Charles Locke
1863–1865	Rev. Joseph Hurst
1864–1865	Rev. Martin Kelly
1864–1865	Rev. James Atkins
1865–1866	Rev. Thomas Rigby
1865–1866	Rev. James Glover
1866–1869	Rev. Edward Woodall
1866–1867	Rev. Alfred Watson
1867–1869	Rev. Edward Walmsley
1868–1879	Rev. Jules de Baere
1869–1874	Rev. Charles Dawson
1870–1875	Rev. Hermann Geurts
1871–1873	Rev. Herbert Duke
1873–1875	Rev. William Wells

1874–1881	Rev. John Hewison
1875–1876	Rev. James Redding
1877–1879	Rev. Charles Parker
1878–1880	Rev. Daniel O'Connell-Harrold
1879–1880	Rev. John Roller
1879–1882	Rev. Gerard de Finance
1880–1881	Rev. Patrick Keating
1881–1882	Rev. John MacDonald
1882–1883	Rev. Henry Shaw
1882–1883	Rev. John Savage
1882–1887	Rev. Cyril Cuypers
1884–1886	Rev. Augustine Collingwood
1886–1888	Rev. Denis O'Sullivan
1887–1888	Rev. William Fenton
1887–1888	Rev. Eugene Daly
1888–1889	Rev. George Sparks
1888–1890	Rev. George Bradley
1888–1896	Rev. Charles Leteux
1889–1893	Rev. Charles Walsh
1891–1893	Rev. Frederick Mitchell
1893–1896	Rev. Michael Mulcahy
1895–1897	Rev. James Cunningham
1896–1899	Rev. John Lea
1896–1913	Rev. Francis van Este
1897–1913	Rev. Emile Callebert
1899–1901	Rev. James Carroll
1901–1902	Rev. William Morrissey
1903–1918	Rev. William Hayes
1913–1914	Rev. Charles Walsh
1913–1920	Rev. William Hudson
1914–1920	Rev. John O'Shea
1915–1930	Rev. Herbert Hudson
1918–1932	Rev. Thomas Molony
1922–1933	Rev. Thomas Watkin
1922–1926	Rev. James Bradley
1927–1936	Rev. Leonard Maudslay
1927–1928	Rev. Stephen Rowland
1930–1933	Rev. Michael McNamara
1933–1934	Rev. Kevin Scannell
1933–1935	Rev. Frederick Mawson
1934–1946	Rev. Austin Hewitt
1935–1946	Rev. Gerard Palframan
1936–1942	Rev. James Clancy
1939–1940	Rev. St John Oram
1939–1940	Rev. Patrick Creed
1940–1942	Rev. Felix Scanlon
1942–1943	Rev. William McShane
1942–1951	Rev. Michael O'Sullivan

1942–1948	Rev. Francis Smith
1943–1946	Rev. Bernard Keegan
1945–1951	Rev. Bernard Jackson
1946–1951	Rev. Nicholas Kennedy
1947–1950	Rev. John Cashman
1951–1954	Rev. Manus Moynihan
1951–1957	Rev. John McGettigan
1951–1955	Rev. Patrick Loftus
1954–1960	Rev. John Murphy
1956–1960	Rev. Terence White
1957–1961	Rev. Peter McGuire
1961–1965	Rev. Gerald Spelman
1961–1962	Rev. Peter Ward
1962–1963	Rev. John O'Hare
1962–1964	Rev. Stephen Sullivan
1963–1968	Rev. John O'Connell
1965–1970	Rev. Owen Brady
1965–1966	Rev. Michael Nealon
1966–1969	Rev. John Raftery
1967–1970	Rev. Peter Grant
1968–1972	Rev. Donal O'Leary
1969–1972	Rev. Peter Ward
1970–1974	Rev. John Roach
1970–1972	Rev. Kevin Martin
1972–1981	Rev. John Grady
1972–1977	Rev. Brendan McKeefry
1974–1977	Rev. Colum Kelly
1976–1982	Rev. John Kinsella
1977–1983	Rev. Peter D. McGuire
1981–1982	Rev. Ignatius de Pont Pujadas
1981–1983	Rev. Augustine O'Reilly
1982–1983	Rev. Denis Haugh
1983–1989	Rev. Eric Newbound
1983–1985	Rev. John Ryan
1985–1988	Rev. Brian Davies
1985–1987	Rev. Craig Elliott
1988–	Rev. William Burgin
1989–	Rev. Brian Gowans

Chaplains of the Home of the Little Sisters of the Poor

1889–1891	Rev. Philip Capron
1891–1892	Rev. George Bradley
1892–1897	Rev. John Brennan
1897–1903	Rev. Patrick Lee
1903–1904	Rev. Michael O'Donnell
1904–1913	Rev. Henry Angenent
1913–1914	Rev. Henry Vos

1914–1919	Rev. Theodore Terken
1919–1929	Rev. Francis Creedon
1929–1931	Rev. John Whitehead
1931–1937	Rev. Thomas Corcoran
1937–1944	Rev. Austin Forkin
1944–1958	Rev. Herbert Hudson
1958–1969	Rev. Leonard Maudslay
1969–1980	Rev. Edward Quinn

Superiors of St Vincent's Mission and Church

1853–1864	Rev. Michael Burke
1864–1882	Rev. Cornelius Hickey
1882–1884	Rev. Daniel O'Sullivan
1884–1889	Rev. James Potter
1889–1892	Rev. Maurice Quish
1892–1897	Rev. John Brady
1897–1906	Rev. Joseph Hanley
1906–1917	Rev. John Conran
1917–1920	Rev. James Bennett
1920–1927	Rev. Patrick Kilty
1927–1933	Rev. Thomas Cleary
1933–1938	Rev. James Bennett
1938–1945	Rev. Christopher O'Leary
1945–1947	Rev. James Thompson
1947–1954	Rev. Joseph McNamara
1954–1963	Rev. Edward McDonagh
1963–1969	Rev. Pierce Gallagher
1969–1974	Rev. Dermot O'Dowd
1974–1977	Rev. Francis McMorrow
1977–1983	Rev. Denis Corkery
1983–1986	Rev. Dermot O'Dowd
1986–1989	Rev. Michael Dunne
1989–	Rev. Hugh McMahon

Assistant Priests

1853–1860	Rev. Thomas Plunkett
1853–1855	Rev. James Kelly
1854–1855	Rev. Michael Gleeson
1855–1860	Rev. Peter Duff
1855–1860	Rev. John Meyers
1857–1883	Rev. James Fitzgerald
1860–1864	Rev. Cornelius Hickey
1860–1865	Rev. Nicholas Barlow
1860–1862	Rev. Patrick McKenna
1862–1863	Rev. Joseph Fischer

1864–1866	Rev. Michael Mullen
1864–1866	Rev. Patrick O'Grady
1866–1868	Rev. Felix McNulty
1866–1872	Rev. Peter Ennis
1872–1873	Rev. Laurence Cahill
1873–1882	Rev. John Stein
1873–1875	Rev. Patrick Campbell
1875–1886	Rev. John Myers
1875–1876	Rev. John Ginouvier
1875–1878	Rev. Christopher Dooley
1875–1889	Rev. Maurice Quish
1877–1886	Rev. Michael Mullen
1878–1879	Rev. Michael Gleeson
1879–1880	Rev. Simon Donovan
1882–1886	Rev. John Hannon
1884–1889	Rev. Edward Gaynor
1886–1890	Rev. Joseph Cussen
1886–1887	Rev. Patrick McNamara
1888–1892	Rev. John Brady
1888–1908	Rev. Eugene Gavin
1889–1890	Rev. Edmund Corcoran
1890–1893	Rev. Michael O'Farrell
1890–1892	Rev. Maurice O'Reilly
1890–1892	Rev. Michael Kiernan
1892–1901	Rev. James Dunphy
1892–1894	Rev. Martin Nolan
1893–1897	Rev. Martin Whitty
1893–1897	Rev. Joseph Hanley
1895–1897	Rev. Joseph Cussen
1896–1897	Rev. Thomas Wickham
1897–1906	Rev. John Brady
1897–1901	Rev. James Rooney
1897–1898	Rev. Maurice Cotter
1898–1903	Rev. Maurice Quish
1898–1899	Rev. John Kelly
1900–1906	Rev. George O'Sullivan
1900–1903	Rev. Edmund Comerford
1900–1903	Rev. James Murray
1902–1912	Rev. James MacDonnell
1903–1905	Rev. Thomas Power
1904–1907	Rev. Patrick Flood
1906–1913	Rev. Robert Jones
1907–1910	Rev. John Boyle
1907–1909	Rev. John Kelly
1907–1911	Rev. Thomas Kickham
1908–1909	Rev. James Rooney
1908–1915	Rev. Patrick Dowling
1908–1909	Rev. Daniel McCarthy

1908–1909	Rev. Maurice Cotter
1909–1911	Rev. Martin Whitty
1909–1911	Rev. Thomas Power
1909–1917	Rev. James Murray
1910–1919	Rev. Charles Bagnall
1911–1919	Rev. Michael Kiernan
1911–1919	Rev. Patrick Hullen
1911–1912	Rev. Michael Gorman
1912–1915	Rev. John Henry
1912–1936	Rev. Nicholas Comerford
1913–1914	Rev. Thomas McCarthy
1913–1924	Rev. Patrick McElligott
1915–1917	Rev. James Bennett
1916–1921	Rev. Gerald Robinson
1917–1919	Rev. Robert Wilson
1919–1925	Rev. Thomas Slavin
1919–1921	Rev. Timothy Manning
1920–1921	Rev. Robert Wilson
1921–1922	Rev. John Russell
1921–1922	Rev. John O'Hanlon
1923–1925	Rev. Daniel McCarthy
1923–1927	Rev. Thomas Cleary
1924–1925	Rev. Thomas Hickey
1924–1926	Rev. Michael Dwyer
1925–1926	Rev. Gerald Robinson
1925–1926	Rev. John Gill
1926–1929	Rev. John Henry
1926–1929	Rev. Michael Twomey
1927–1930	Rev. Patrick Bannigan
1928–1929	Rev. Gerald Robinson
1928–1930	Rev. Vincent Allen
1929–1938	Rev. Christopher O'Leary
1929–1934	Rev. Joseph McDonald
1929–1939	Rev. Michael Heron
1930–1935	Rev. Gerard Tierney
1930–1932	Rev. Edward Conran
1934–1940	Rev. Patrick Barry
1934–1937	Rev. Edward Conran
1934–1945	Rev. Patrick Gilgunn
1934–1935	Rev. Thomas Finnigan
1935–1947	Rev. Daniel O'Connell
1937–1943	Rev. Gerard Galligan
1937–1954	Rev. Edward McDonagh
1938–1939	Rev. John Gill
1939–1949	Rev. Michael Devlin
1939–1947	Rev. Joseph McNamara
1939–1947	Rev. Owen McArdle
1940–1943	Rev. James O'Brien

1943–1945	Rev. Edmund O'Hanlon
1943–1949	Rev. John Oakey
1945–1949	Rev. Michael Doyle
1945–1948	Rev. James McCarthy
1945–1948	Rev. Patrick Brady
1945–1947	Rev. Francis Cleere
1945–1947	Rev. Daniel O'Connell
1947–1949	Rev. Michael Howard
1947–1949	Rev. Henry Morrin
1947–1981	Rev. Gerard Galligan
1947–1981	Rev. Kevin O'Hagan
1948–1949	Rev. Maurice Kavanagh
1949–1952	Rev. Patrick Bannigan
1949–1952	Rev. Thomas Lyng
1949–1955	Rev. John O'Hare
1949–1956	Rev. Thomas O'Farrell
1949–1953	Rev. Robert Towers-Perkins
1949–1950	Rev. Thomas Smyth
1950–1955	Rev. William Meagher
1950–1953	Rev. Francis Cleere
1950–1957	Rev. Thomas Rice
1952–1954	Rev. Michael Mannix
1952–1953	Rev. Michael Bennet
1953–1954	Rev. John N. Smyth
1953–1963	Rev. Edmund McGlinchy
1954–1957	Rev. Daniel O'Connell
1954–1957	Rev. Kevin Murnaghan
1954–1956	Rev. Michael Heron
1954–1959	Rev. Arthur McRory
1954–1961	Rev. Thomas Finnigan
1955–1964	Rev. Denis Corkery
1956–1957	Rev. James Rooney
1957–1958	Rev. Michael Mannix
1957–1967	Rev. John Murphy
1958–1966	Rev. Denis Collins
1958–1959	Rev. Robert Towers-Perkins
1959–1967	Rev. Kevin Murnaghan
1959–1963	Rev. Pierce Gallagher
1961–1964	Rev. Kevin Scallon
1963–1964	Rev. Michael Doyle
1963–1966	Rev. Michael Walsh
1963–1967	Rev. Desmond MacMorrow
1964–1965	Rev. Patrick Hughes
1964–1968	Rev. James McQuillan
1965–1973	Rev. Hugh McMahon
1966–1968	Rev. Bernard Buckley
1967–1968	Rev. John Hurley
1967–1969	Rev. Anthony McDonnell

1966–1968	Rev. Eamon Cowan
1968–1983	Rev. James Dyar
1969–1971	Rev. Thomas O'Farrell
1969–1971	Rev. William Murphy
1969–1970	Rev. John Walshe
1971–1973	Rev. Michael Walsh
1971–1977	Rev. Raymond Armstrong
1977–1978	Rev. Denis Collins
1978–1982	Rev. Patrick Hughes
1981–	Rev. Michael Walsh
1982–1984	Rev. Cornelius Curtin
1984–1989	Rev. Hugh McMahon
1989–	Rev. Charles Gardner

Vincentian Lay Brothers

1853–1862	Bro. John Bradley
1962–1909	Bro. Timothy O'Donnell
1892–1931	Bro. Michael Murphy
1929–	Bro. William Smith

University Chaplains

1952–1961	Rev. Gerard Shannon, CM
1961–1967	Rev. Terence J. Corrigan
1967–1978	Rev. Joseph A. Smith
1978–1982	Rev. David W. Barnes
1982–1990	Rev. Giles Hibbert, OP
1990–	Rev. Peter Cullen

Fr Donald Stoker served as chaplain to the Sheffield Polytechnic College from 1974 to 1981.

Rectors of St William's Church

1932–1952	Rev. Thomas Molony
1952–1961	Rev. Diarmuid Scannell
1961–	Rev. Thomas Keegan

Assistant Priests

1938–1940	Rev. Donal Murray
1940–1952	Rev. John Kearns
1952–1954	Rev. Michael Grace
1954–1959	Rev. Charles Hadfield
1959–1961	Rev. Michael Killeen

Chaplains of the Polish Catholic Centre

1950–1978	Rev. Michael Szymankiewicz
1978–1986	Rev. Stanislaw Cymbalista
1986–	Rev. Stanislaw Tylka

Rectors of the Sacred Heart Church

1920–1946	Rev. Robert Dunford
1946–1955	Rev. John Mitchell
1955–1965	Rev. James Farrel
1965–	Rev. Michael O'Sullivan

Assistant Priests

1922–1923	Rev. John Colgan
1923–1925	Rev. Matthew Dunne
1925–1927	Rev. Thomas Donovan
1927–1932	Rev. John Flynn
1932–1938	Rev. William Backhouse
1937–1940	Rev. Frederick Mawson
1938–1941	Rev. Kieron Kehoe
1940–1946	Rev. William Daly
1946–1952	Rev. Benedict McCabe
1946–1953	Rev. Donald Backhouse
1952–1958	Rev. Andrew Daly
1953–1957	Rev. Anthony Farrar
1958–1963	Rev. Denis Tangney
1963–1968	Rev. Daniel O'Keeffe
1968–1973	Rev. Hubert McNamara
1974–1976	Rev. Augustine O'Reilly
1975–1980	Rev. Laurence Hulme
1980–1982	Rev. Joseph Long
1982–1985	Rev. Martin Williams
1985–1988	Rev. Hubert McNamara
1988–1989	Rev. Andrew Brown
1989–	Rev. John Sharp

Chaplains of the Carmelite Convent, Kirkedge

1911–1914	Rev. Theodore Terken
1914–1929	Rev. Joseph McAuliffe
1929–1931	Rev. James Reynolds
1931–1937	Rev. Austin Forkin
1937–1943	Served from the Sacred Heart

1943–1947   Rev. Thomas Brady
1947–1952   Rev. Jerome O'Sullivan

Rectors of St Charles's Church

1864–1866   Rev. Martin Kelly
1866–1905   Rev. Joseph Hurst
1905–1908   Rev. Martin Adams
1908–1934   Rev. Michael Beazley
1934–1944   Rev. Lawrence Gallon
1944–1953   Rev. Francis Moverley
1953–1963   Rev. Joseph Stoker
1963–1967   Rev. Columba Mullan
1967–1980   Rev. Patrick Higgins
1980–   Rev. Peter Moran

Assistant Priests

1899–1905   Rev. Martin Adams
1905–1906   Rev. Michael Bradley
1906–1907   Rev. Jeremiah O'Sullivan
1907–1915   Rev. Thomas McEnery
1915–1917   Rev. Patrick Kane
1917–1923   Rev. John Whitehead
1923–1932   Rev. Lawrence Gallon
1932–1944   Rev. Patrick Bradley
1944–1950   Rev. George Hinchcliffe
1950–1954   Rev. Bernard Battle
1954–1960   Rev. Eugene Daly
1960–1961   Rev. Alexander Cavanagh
1961–1964   Rev. Kevin Meeds
1964–1968   Rev. Stephen Sullivan

Rectors of St Joseph's Church

1869–1870   Rev. Henry Formby
1870–1875   Rev. Theophilus van Cauwenberghe
1875–1922   Rev. Adrian van Roosmalen
1922–1939   Rev. Arthur Kay
1939–1965   Rev. Timothy Moynihan
1965–1975   Rev. William McShane
1975–1984   Rev. Michael Keegan
1984–   Rev. Gerald White

Assistant Priests

1919–1920	Rev. Timothy Moynihan
1920–1922	Rev. Arthur Kay
1938–1947	Rev. Richard Caterall
1941–1946	Rev. William Bryson
1941–1942	Rev. Michael Connelly
1946–1952	Rev. John Rutledge
1952–1954	Rev. Thomas Maudslay
1954–1958	Rev. Edward Woodhouse
1958–1963	Rev. Andrew Daly
1963–1964	Rev. Bernard Battle
1964–1967	Rev. Peter Ward
1967–1969	Rev. Michael Conlin
1969–1972	Rev. Sylvester O'Donnell
1971–1973	Rev. Thomas Dunne
1972–1974	Rev. Philip Holroyd
1973–1976	Rev. William Delaney
1974–1977	Rev. Patrick Keohane
1977–1979	Rev. John Metcalfe
1982–1984	Rev. Ignatius de Pont Pujadas

Rectors of St Catherine's Church

1876–1902	Rev. Luke Burke
1902–1921	Rev. Patrick Hickey
1921–1958	Rev. John White
1958–1968	Rev. Edward Ward
1968–1973	Rev. Patrick Loftus
1973–1979	Rev. John Quirke
1979–1981	Rev. Peter Moran
1981–1989	Rev. Reginald Bessler
1989–	Rev. Donald Stoker

Assistant Priests

1899–1903	Rev. Robert Noonan
1903–1904	Rev. Henry Angenent
1904–1906	Rev. Michael O'Donnell
1906–1907	Rev. William Dobson
1907–1910	Rev. John O'Shea
1910–1913	Rev. William Hudson
1913–1919	Rev. Thomas Byrne
1919–1924	Rev. James Kavanagh
1924–1930	Rev. Charles Daly
1926–1929	Rev. George Grogan

1929–1934	Rev. Bernard Blackburn
1934–1937	Rev. Thomas Brady
1937–1939	Rev. Eustace Malone
1939–1948	Rev. Denis McMahon
1939–1943	Rev. Michael Brennan
1943–1945	Rev. Hugh O'Neill
1945–1952	Rev. Daniel McDyer
1948–1950	Rev. Cornelius Finn
1950–1954	Rev. Patrick Henry
1952–1958	Rev. Patrick Higgins
1954–1960	Rev. Thomas Kenny
1958–1963	Rev. Vincent O'Hara
1960–1964	Rev. Leonard Spencer
1963–1966	Rev. Kevin Martin
1964–1969	Rev. Gerald Hargreaves
1966–1969	Rev. David Armitage
1968–1973	Rev. John McNamee
1969–1971	Rev. Maurice Keenan
1971–1973	Rev. Michael Grogan
1973–1982	Rev. Kieran O'Connell
1979–1980	Rev. Patrick Hegarty
1982–1985	Rev. Anthony Attree
1985–1986	Rev. Stanley Roberts
1986–	Rev. William Fitzpatrick, CSSp

Rectors of St Patrick's Church

1930–1943	Rev. Bernard Ford
1943–1951	Rev. Lawrence Gallon
1951–1965	Rev. George Collins
1965–1970	Rev. James Flavin
1970–	Rev. Michael Daly

Assistant Priests

1934–1937	Rev. Joseph Stoker
1937–1946	Rev. Bernard Benson
1942–1946	Rev. Francis Holland
1943–1944	Rev. Louis Heston
1944–1946	Rev. James Quinn
1946–1948	Rev. Donald Backhouse
1946–1952	Rev. Joseph Lyons
1948–1953	Rev. Donal Banbury
1952-1956	Rev. James O'Flynn
1953–1955	Rev. Patrick Healy
1955–1956	Rev. Edward Horkin
1956–1957	Rev. John Crissell

1956–1961	Rev. John Morrissey
1957–1958	Rev. Bernard Ineson
1961–1966	Rev. Kevin Griffin
1966–1968	Rev. Barrie Holmes
1968–1969	Rev. Sean Creaton
1969–1970	Rev. John McGuinness
1970–1975	Rev. Patrick Henry
1974–1979	Rev. Eugene McGillicuddy
1975–1978	Rev. Kenneth Taylor
1978–1984	Rev. Patrick Walsh
1979–1981	Rev. Arthur Wrightson
1984–1987	Rev. Terence Doherty
1987–	Rev. Desmond Sexton

Rectors of St Thomas More's Church

1945–1956	Rev. Francis Holland
1956–1982	Rev. Thomas O'Reilly
1982–1989	Rev. Andrew Daly
1989–	Rev. Bernard Bedford

Assistant Priests

1951–1955	Rev. John Jackson
1955–1959	Rev. Michael Killeen
1959–1960	Rev. Peter Dean
1960–1964	Rev. John Collins
1964–1970	Rev. Peter Hurley
1970–1975	Rev. Joseph Taylor
1975–1982	Rev. Peter Kirkham
1985–1986	Rev. Michael Connelly

Rectors of the Church of the Mother of God

1879–1890	Rev. Julius de Baere
1890–1892	Rev. James Glover
1892–1940	Rev. George Bradley
1940–1957	Rev. Michael Dunleavy
1957–1978	Rev. Patrick Falvey
1978–	Rev. William Kilgannon

Assistant Priests

1907–1908	Rev. Thomas Bradley
1940–1942	Rev. William Cavanagh
1942–1945	Rev. John Convery

1945–1946	Rev. Patrick Roche
1945–1949	Rev. Vincent Cuffe
1946–1951	Rev. John Casey
1949–1952	Rev. Austin Roddy
1952–1956	Rev. John Hudson
1953–1954	Rev. Bernard Blackburn
1953–1954	Rev. Patrick Creed
1956–1960	Rev. Joseph Kearns
1960–1963	Rev. Bernard Leonard
1963–1967	Rev. John Roach
1967–1970	Rev. Brendan McKeefry
1970–1972	Rev. John Grady
1972–1974	Rev. Paul Lyons
1975–1978	Rev. John Metcalfe
1977–1978	Rev. William Kilgannon
1978–1982	Rev. Anthony Attree
1982–1985	Rev. Thomas Durkin
1985–1986	Rev. David Kirkwood
1989–	Rev. Brian Gowans

Rectors of Holy Family Church

1954–1955	Rev. Patrick Creed
1955–1958	Rev. Joseph Telford
1958–1964	Rev. William Kelly
1964–1968	Rev. Francis Pepper
1968–1977	Rev. Henry Townend
1977–1981	Rev. Kevin Thornton
1981–1990	Rev. Kevin O'Hagan, CM

Rectors of Our Lady and St Thomas's Church

1911–1913	Rev. Henry Hunt
1913–1942	Rev. James Rooney
1942–1954	Rev. Arthur Bird
1954–1958	Rev. James Kavanagh
1958–1990	Rev. Emil Puttmann
1990–	Rev. Gerald Burke

Assistant Priests

1954–1956	Rev. Patrick McKay
1956–1959	Rev. Vincent Rush
1959–1962	Rev. Bernard Doran
1962–1966	Rev. John Mack
1966–1970	Rev. Eugene O'Mahony

1970–1971	Rev. Eamonn O'Hara
1971–1974	Rev. Eric Tinker
1974–1978	Rev. Francis Daly
1978–1982	Rev. Bernard Bedford
1982–1984	Rev. John Kinsella
1984–1985	Rev. Peter Cullen
1985–1986	Rev. Michael O'Connor
1986–1988	Rev. Andrew Graydon
1988–	Rev. Charles Neal

Rectors of St Theresa's Church

1934–1935	Rev. George Grogan
1935–1974	Rev. Denis McGillicuddy
1974–1979	Rev. Eugene Daly
1979–1990	Rev. Patrick O'Connor
1990–	Rev. Brian Davies

Assistant Priests

1942–1945	Rev. Andrew Hegarty
1943–1952	Rev. Michael Daly
1949–1954	Rev. Timothy Feely
1952–1956	Rev. John Knox
1954–1960	Rev. Patrick Langan
1960–1965	Rev. Maurice Keenan
1961–1967	Rev. Patrick O'Keeffe
1965–1972	Rev. James Shryane
1967–1971	Rev. Laurence Lister
1971–1974	Rev. Peter Hurley
1972–1975	Rev. Adrian Smith
1974–1981	Rev. James Kennedy
1975–1977	Rev. Edward O'Connor
1981–1982	Rev. John Grady
1984–1986	Rev. William Fitzpatrick, CSSp
1986–1988	Rev. Ian Hall
1988–1990	Rev. Brian Davies

Rectors of St Oswald's Church

1948–1953	Rev. Gerard Palframan
1953–1966	Rev. John Kearns
1966–1980	Rev. John Horan
1980–1985	Rev. Patrick Higgins
1985–1990	Rev. Peter Cullen

Assistant Priests

1949–1953	Rev. Matthew Farrelly
1953–1958	Rev. Leonard May

Between 1964 and 1970 Fr Thomas Hartnett, OSA, did extended supply work here and at St William's and St Joseph's, Handsworth. In 1990 a community of the Marist Order was appointed to St Oswald's church, consisting of Fr Desmond Hanrahan, SM, Fr Peter Murray, SM, and Bro Ivan Vodopivec, SM.

Rectors of Our Lady of Lourdes Church

1953–1970	Rev. Peter McDonagh
1970–1982	Rev. Oliver Wilson
1982–1989	Rev. Bernard Bedford
1989–	Rev. Martin Williams

Assistant Priests

1958–1963	Rev. Anthony O'Dowd
1963–1965	Rev. William Walsh
1965–1968	Rev. Ronald Brown
1968–1969	Rev. Patrick Murphy
1970–1973	Rev. John Gilroy, CSSp
1973–1977	Rev. Denis Higgins
1977–1982	Rev. Denis Hough
1983–1984	Rev. Leslie Roberts

Rectors of the Church of St Francis

1968–1982	Rev. Ronald Fox
1982–	Rev. Michael Killeen

BIBLIOGRAPHY

1. Primary Works

1a. *MS and Pictorial Sources*

Sheffield City Library:
    Arundel Castle Manuscripts, S (Sheffield) and D (Derbyshire).
    Diary of William Statham (1694–1734).
    St Vincent's Presbytery, Builder's Specifications.
    Seven plans of the Catholic Chapel, 1838.
    Barbara Cassidy, A History of Sheffield's Roman Catholic Schools, typescript, 1969.
    Norah Geraghty, A Short History of the Parish of St Wilfrid and the Mother of God, Sheffield, typescript, 1980.
    Stephen Welsh, Notes on the architectural firm of J.G. Weightman and M.E. Hadfield.
Archives of the English Province SJ, Farm Street:
    Ralph Baines, Manuscript History of Spinkhill.
Hallam Diocesan Curia:
    Account Book of Canon Fisher.
Ushaw College:
    Robert Tate Correspondence.

1b. *Periodicals*
Architect and Building News, 1926–1971.
Architectural Review, 1896–.
British Archaeological Association Journal, 1874–.
British Architect, 1874–1919.
The Builder, 1843–
Builders' Journal, 1895–1910; thereafter *Architects' and Builders' Journal*, 1910–1919; thereafter *Architects' Journal*, 1919–.
Building News, 1855–1926; thereafter amalgamated with *The Architect*..
Catholic Annual Register, 1850.
Catholic Building Review, 1956–.
Catholic Directory of England and Wales, 1838–.
Catholic Education Council Handbook, 1960–1988.
Catholic Record Society transactions, 1904–.
Catholic Voice, 1982–1989.
Church Building, 1960–.
The Dublin Builder, 1859–1866.
Hallam Diocesan Year Book, 1981–.
Hallam News, 1989–.
The Hallamshire Catholic, 1937–1944.
Laity's Directory, 1799–1837.

St Marie's Catholic Monthly.
Sheffield and Rotherham Independent, 1839–1901.
Sheffield Illustrated, 1885.
Sheffield Telegraph, 1855–1967; thereafter *Morning Telegraph* to 1986.
The Tablet, 1840–.
Telegraph and Star, 1937–1938; thereafter *The Star*.

2. Secondary Works

2a. *Monographs, Biographies, etc.*
Anstruther, G., *The Seminary Priests* (4 vols.; Great Wakering: Mayhew McCrimmon, 1968–1977).
Calendar of State Papers, Scotland, vol. II (Edinburgh: HM General Register Office, 1900).
Catalogue of the Arundel Castle Manuscripts (Sheffield: Libraries and Arts Committee, 1965).
Colvin, H., *Biographical Dictionary of British Architects* (London: John Murray, 2nd edn; 1978).
de l'Hôpital, W., *Westminster Cathedral and Its Architect* (2 vols.; London: Hutchinson, 1919).
Dictionary of National Biography (London: Smith, Elder and Company, 1885–).
Eastlake, C., *A History of the Gothic Revival* (London: Longmans, Green, 1872).
Foley, H., *Records of the English Province SJ* (8 vols.; London: Burns and Oates, 1877–1883).
Foundations of the Sisters of Notre Dame (Liverpool: Philip, Son and Nephew, 1895).
Fraser, A., *Mary Queen of Scots* (London: Weidenfeld and Nicolson, 1969).
Gatty, A., *Sheffield Past and Present* (Sheffield: Clark and Greenup, 1873).
Gillow, J., *Bibliographical Dictionary of the English Catholics* (5 vols.; London: Burns and Oates, 1885–1898).
Hadfield, C., *A History of St Marie's Mission and Church, Sheffield* (Sheffield: Pawson and Brailsford, 1889).
Hibbert, C., *King Mob: The Story of Lord George Gordon and the London Riots of 1780* (London: Longmans, Green, 1958).
Hunter, J., *Hallamshire* (London: Virtue, 1975).
Kelly, B.W., *Historical Notes on English Catholic Missions* (London: Kegan Paul, Trench, Trubner, 1907).
Leader, J.D., *Mary Queen of Scots in Captivity* (Sheffield: Leader, 1880).
Leader, R.E., *Sheffield in the Eighteenth Century* (Sheffield: The Sheffield Independent Press, 1901).
Odom, W., *Mary Stuart, Queen of Scots* (London: George Bell; Sheffield: J.W. Northend, 1904).
O'Hara, I. and C. O'Hara, *St Joseph's Handsworth 1881–1981* (Sheffield: St Joseph's Church, 1981).
Pevsner, N., *The Buildings of England: Yorkshire, West Riding* (Harmondsworth: Penguin, 2nd edn; 1967).
Plumb, B., *Arundel to Zabi: A Biographical Dictionary of the Catholic Bishops of England and Wales (Deceased) 1623–1987* (Warrington: Brian Plumb, 1987).
Pugin, A.W.N., *The Present State of Ecclesiastical Architecture in England* (London: Dolman, 1843).
Records of the Scots Colleges (Aberdeen: New Spalding Club, 1906).
Robinson, J.M., *The Dukes of Norfolk: A Quincentennial History* (Oxford: Oxford University Press, 1982).
Sacred Heart Church, 1936–1986, Golden Jubilee (Sheffield: Sacred Heart Church, 1986).

St Francis of Assisi, Sandygate, Ceremony of Consecration (Sheffield: St Francis Church, 1989).

St Patrick's School Golden Jubilee (Sheffield: St Patrick's Church, 1977).

St Patrick's, Sheffield, Golden Jubilee 1939–1989 (Sheffield: St Patrick's Church, 1989).

St Peter's School, Handbook of Opening (Sheffield: St Peter's School, 1959).

St Thomas More, Sheffield (Sheffield: St Thomas More Church, 1969).

St Vincent's Sheffield, 1853–1953 (Sheffield: St Vincent's Church, 1953).

Souvenir of the Solemn Opening of St Theresa's New Church, Sheffield (Sheffield: St Theresa's Church, 1960).

Strickland, A., *Life of Mary Queen of Scots* (2 vols.; London: G. Bell, 1873).

Sullivan, S.P. and J. Ryan, *St Marie's Cathedral, A History and Guide* (Leominster: Fowler Wright Books, 1988).

Sweeney, G., *A Pilgrim's Guide to Padley* (Nottingham: Diocese of Nottingham, 1978).

Taaffe, W., *Our Lady and St Thomas, Sheffield, 1932–1982* (Sheffield: Our Lady and St Thomas Church, 1982).

Vickers, J.E., *100 Years of Worship 1883–1983* (Sheffield: Abbeydale Congregational Church, 1983).

Walton, M., *Sheffield, Its Story and Its Achievements* (Sheffield: The Sheffield Telegraph, 1952).

Watkin, E.I., *Roman Catholicism in England* (London: Oxford University Press, 1957).

White, J., *St Catherine's Church, Sheffield 1876–1936 Jubilee Memento* (Sheffield: St Catherine's Church, 1936).

Worall, E.S., *Returns of Papists 1767* (London: Catholic Record Society, 1989).

2b. *Articles*

Burns, T.H.,'Catholicism in Defeat', *History Today* (Nov. 1966), pp. 790-93.

Field, M., 'Life in Sheffield 300 Years Ago', *The Star* (25 Nov. 1980).

Isherwood, K., 'Church Sculpture', *The Studio* (Feb. 1952), pp. 44-45.

Pollen, J.H., 'Mary Stuart's Jesuit Chaplain', *The Month*, Jan. and Feb. 1911.

Stienlet, V., 'St Francis of Assisi, Crosspool', *Church Building* (Spring 1990), pp. 39-44.

Supple, J., 'The Role of the Catholic Laity in Yorkshire, 1850–1900', *Recusant History* 18 (May 1987), pp. 304-17.

—'Ultramontism in Yorkshire 1850–1900', *Recusant History* 17 (May 1985), pp. 274-86.

INDEX

INDEX OF PRIESTS

GENERAL INDEX